EMPOWERING GURUS

SUMATHI KULKARNI

Become
Shakespeare
.com

First published in 2020 by
BecomeShakespeare.com

One Point Six Technologies Pvt. Ltd.
Office No. 119-123, 1st Floor,
Building J2, B - Wing,
WadalaTruck Terminal, Wadala East, Mumbai,
Maharashtra, India, 400022.
T: +91 8080226699

ISBN: 978-93-90463-01-5

PREFACE

GURU THE TEACHER

गुरुर्ब्रम्हा गुरु विष्णू:
गुरु:देवो महेश्वरा।
गुरु: साक्षात् परं ब्रह्म
तस्मै श्री गुरुवे नमः।।

Guru Brahma Guru Vishnu Guru Devo Maheshwarah

Guru Saakshaat Para brahma

Tasmai Shri Guruveh Namaha

Tasmai ShriGuruveh Namaha

Meaning: *The guru is the creator, the guru is the preserver, and the guru is the destroyer. The guru is the absolute. I bow before you.*

Guru is our teacher. In our culture Guru is placed on the highest pedestal and is respected above all.

Teaching is a noble profession. Teacher is supposed to be the model of the absolute in the eyes of every student. The belief in providing professional assistance to the builders of the nation "TEACHERS" who have embraced teaching profession is very strong in India. Why not? The enrichment and empowerment programme is for teachers with a passion for teaching. How far we are successful, is a matter of introspection.

The school is built on four pillars. **Management, Teachers, Parents and Children are four pillars.** Though comprehensively speaking all pillars have equal responsibility in conducting affairs of a school, here we are dealing with one of the main components ie teachers who are the ones who activate the whole school for reaching its objectives for a better future of the children and the citizens at large.

In a snap judgement a leading news paper had published this *"The failure of 99% candidates who took the Central Teacher Eligibility Test, which was introduced to improve the quality of teaching in schools, points to the abysmal standards of B Ed degree courses. No wonder our students end up at the bottom end of global student assessment rankings. Add to that students scoring 99% marks but failing to get college admission, and our education system is truly bizarre."*

<u>OBJECTIVE</u>: This pointedly questions the system and its relevance to motivation of students and teachers in their study and profession respectively. This also questions the quality and standards of educational degrees and motivation for those students who don't get college admission in spite of doing extremely well.

It is to develop an indispensable bridge between teacher motivations and enhancement of quality education. It is very essential to improve their skills in motivation and widen their knowledge. There are three essential factors to be considered to overall development of quality teachers. Specific subjects should have a systematic orientation. It should be in an organised as well as methodical direction. Techniques used by the teachers should be subject specific and consist of innovative methodologies. Teachers should be strengthened, empowered, provided with best environment to take initiatives for innovative and creative work. Steps should be taken to manage and arrange orientation workshops in pedagogy which will be subject wise presentation or subject specific. These workshops be focused at both new entrants as well as for in-service teachers. These piece meal recipes should serve the teachers to get acquainted with the latest available technology. There should be specially designed programmes put in order for fresh as well as experienced teachers directed towards this objective. Both these new entrants and in-service teachers should be made aware of use of IT related techniques of teachings.

There is a normal tendency of teachers not inclined towards participating in seminars, symposia, workshops etc. There should be steps in line for teachers' encouragement and motivation to enthusiastically participate in such gatherings of learning.

"I was working in a school which adopted a different kind of approach to Pre-primary teachers. The challenge was, none of their tiny tots should come to school crying. The motivation from the management was so strong for pre-primary teachers that they would feel happy when tiny tots would ask their parents to go back and they would in turn happily join their friends and teachers of their class."

Such should be the motivation for teachers to join these knowledgeable and purposeful assemblies of teachers.

PROLOGUE

<u>MOULDING A CHILD</u>

A baby is a gift of nature. Whether it is a baby plant, animal or a human baby, in a unique way represents God or nature in its purest form. That is how we instantly fall in love with a baby. The nature is ingrained with the quality of growth or development or change. Thus 'change' a natural phenomenon is in nature continuously struggling to take different forms and shapes. A child grows out of a baby. A child is a bundle of the finest qualities at the subtlest level. To bring these unmanifest characteristics to their manifestations is a gradual process. A flower to blossom on a plant happens only in due course of time, under certain care and conditions. Every child needs a mother's love and a father's guidance. Only a Guru's blessings can complete it. That is where the importance of teacher arises. The fact that the child takes our attention, energy, time and a part of our life to make its place in this space and time goes to prove that a teacher's contribution in the development of the child is undeniable.

A child is a symbol of life in its vigorous form. Children are playful and contribute to the spirit in life, children are boundless in thoughts and thus contribute to thinking beyond, children are stress busters and so enjoy themselves and make the others around them totally involved, help keep away from the tensions at least temporarily. They are isolated springs of energies in various colours, hues and tastes. They pour a lot of positive energy around to make life lighter and easier. It is very much acceptable when a few teachers give an otherwise view of the children's overflowing energy as troublesome and draining. But when the same children come to you with lot of love, a sorry figure and an apology without many words, it's a feeling of an achievement that is beyond even Alexander's victory. Reward of love, strong emotional support and one to one positive rapport with the most troublesome children certainly works wonders. These are the basic needs if provided at appropriate time and in right situations the children are there with you for everything that a teacher asks for. Then the bothersome situations are rightly controlled on their own. Teaching and learning process becomes a smooth and enjoyable ride.

A child, whether mischievous or well behaved, is totally focused on the teacher. A sensitive or an experienced teacher doesn't miss any chance to bring in any kind of change that is required for the positive development of the child. The rapport that is to be built, is the first and the foremost, the rest follows naturally. But how many of us enjoy doing it? And that is supposed to be the essential part of the school and the teaching and learning process, academics comes later. Once the child settles within the purview of psychological security provided by the teacher it becomes easier, enjoyable and productive for the teacher as the hurdles dissolve and the initiative begins from the child in the learning process contributing to the learning process productively. The child centered teaching and learning dawns and makes learning more fruitful and permanent.

Thus a teacher moulds a child, polishes his or her being and provides opportunities to the emotional and intellectual growth through the years. Once these faculties are irrigated with proper information and knowledge through right canalization, the growth of the child is in the right direction. The policy of a school should hold to prepare the child with all the skills to face the future. Total personality development is a tool, which a child carries from his or her school – confidence, awareness, physique, skills, information and academics – to be able to lead a life as a complete human being and an aware citizen of a country in the decades to come.

ABOUT THE AUTHOR

I am a teacher with more than 25 years of teaching experience, with a Post Graduate degree in English, a PG teaching certificate and a PG diploma in teaching English from EFLU (English and Foreign Languages University).

A few of my write ups have been published in News papers, Femina, Frozen Thoughts and a couple of Defence Magazines.

I am from a defence background with my husband just retired as a colonel. I have a married daughter working at Benguluru.

I have about 38 topics written for my book which include essays, narratives, imaginative, poems, factual etc and was a collection under the title **"Bouquet of Brainwaves"** published in 2013.

My second book is **"A Tale of Two Dogs in STRING OF PEARLS"** was a collection of poems published in 2017.

This is my third book dedicated to the noble profession of teaching and the makers of human beings out of naive and youthful children. It deals with child centred education to begin with, extending to application of Information and Communication Technology and bringing in the essential role of Creativity, Value based Approach and Constructive Deviation in dealing with application of comprehensive teaching in the Education System.

ACKNOWLEDGEMENT

I am indebted to Mr Jayaprakash sir of Rishi Valley School and Mr Yogendra Guruwara sir of Sherwood and Heritage Valley Schools for all that I learnt under their guidance in promoting teaching and learning strategies in schools. This learning in a decade of teaching is interspersed, sprinkled and scattered in the form of thoughts and ideas expressed throughout the book. I extend my heartfelt gratitude to them.

CHAPTER INDEX

FOREWORD

<u>TEACHING PHILOSOPHY</u>

मातृ देवो भव।

पितृ देवो भव।

आचार्य देवो भव।

अतिथि देवो भव।।

Matru devo bhavah,

Pitru devo bhavah,

Acharya devo bhavah.

Atithi devo bhavah.

गुरुर्ब्रम्हा गुरुविष्णू: गुरु:र्देवो महेश्वरा । गुरु: साक्षात् परं ब्रह्म तस्मै श्री गुरुवे नमः।।

Guru Brahma, Guru Vishnu, Guru devo Maheshwara.

Guru sakshat para Brahma, Tasmai shri Guruvennamaha.

The above sloka is from Tittiriya Upanishad which has been originated from vedic era and is a part of our vedas written thousands of years ago and is relevant even today. The Vedas tell us that immediately after mother and father, comes the teacher. Teacher is at par with Brahma, Vishnu and Maheshwara. I bow to him.

A child is a unique creation of nature. A child is like a seed; With rain, sunlight and fertile land, the seed grows into a plant and a tree. The nature nurtures it with a lot of care and love, albeit invisible sometimes. The latest trend in teaching a child without either physical or mental abuse effortlessly breeds the warmth of love everywhere. Interacting with a child on any information or knowledge with an engulfing aura of love makes it easy to handle the teaching sessions.

Mingling with the students and creating an understanding, an atmosphere of fearless based on an affectionate rapport are essential for the perfect exchange of ideas and opinions. It is very necessary that the students and their feelings be treated sensitively. Every child is valued for what she is and due importance given to each child. Every child is a unique creation of God. It is important to correct her mistakes without hurting the child's feelings and thus creating a positive rapport with child's feelings.

The main job of the teacher as a facilitator is to provide a child with maximum opportunity to come out with her ideas, opinions and suggestions and not to forget the questions. Creation of a genuine thirst for knowledge by raising inquiries should be the goal.

Group work and discussions are great platforms. Fear and shyness should be slowly but surely erased from a child's mind. They are blockades in the flow of thought and expression. The technique of physical punishments used in teaching must be discarded. The effectiveness of teaching with love is total and deep compared to teaching by punishment.

SECTION – I
The Philosophy of Teaching

1.
CHILD CENTERED TEACHING

To begin with, an honest endeavor should be to teach a child and see that individual attention is paid, so that learning happens. In the process, we need to discover the child's needs, abilities, talent and give ample opportunities for all-round development so that she grows into a complete human being. We need to look at comprehensive growth and make an attempt at progress and expansion with an all inclusive personality.

- Teacher-centred: Teacher dominated and teacher centric teaching and learning. This is also known as curriculum centred.

- Child-centred: Here it is the child who is of main concern and center of learning and teaching. This is also known as Learner-centred.

- This mostly depends on your individual style your teaching. Some of the elements that could influence are as:

  ❖ Layout of the classroom.

  ❖ How you prepare for your teaching.

  ❖ Number of activities used.

  ❖ Types of activities used.

  ❖ How learner uses your methods.

Teacher centered:

This is the most common and traditional way of teaching which was dominant throughout the world over the years. This was assumed to be the only way of teaching. The teacher would dispel the information on a subject in front of students without knowing whether the student has understood or not.

It was assumed that a teacher was perfect in the subject and whatever he or she said was gospel, accepted without any dissonance.

- No questions to be asked.

- Students who understood were lucky.

- Those who did not understand were left to their fate.

- The teacher would do her or his part by taking a lesson.

- It was one sided teaching.

- The purpose was to complete the syllabus.

- The goal was to learn by heart and reproduce in the test or examination.

In due course of time, these assumptions were proved to be incorrect, unacceptable and insufficient for a student to understand and learn a topic or a concept. And thus, these assumptions were looked down upon and the child was given the most important place in teaching and learning concepts. Thus evolved teaching processes and two essential ways, means or techniques came into existence as follows.

Child-centered: Teaching and learning revolves round the child.

Subject-centered: Teaching and learning revolves round the subject.

Child-centered teaching is complemented by a child friendly environment.

The child should be treated as an individual who is able to do anything and is competent, accomplished, talented, proficient, skilled and gifted. **Motivation** is what is needed that makes them work towards studying.

They should be made to realise the utlity of what they are learning and the rest would be taken care of.

Child is the centre of the whole process. Teacher's teaching concepts revolve round the child until the goal is achieved. The purpose of learning has to be reached. Child is the centre of attraction that is to be served with all ways until he understands. Use any means of teaching and learning but ultimately the child's understanding of the concept, topic or story has to be complete.

The Ssbject centred approach focuses on the subject, leaving the learner or the child in the periphery. In this process, student or child is nowhere brought in to the picture. We find the teacher involved in the subject to be continuously present in the scene. Sometimes both teacher and the subject are so prominent that the learner's role is completely ignored. It is like honk, honk and only honking on the subject to the extent that the children are silent and passive participants. The teachers are usually blissfully unaware of this fact. Regardless of whether the subject is being taught impressively. The truth of the matter is that the child's mental participation is completely unknown and uncared for.

As it is clearly visible in the above illustration the link between the given factors of:

- CHILD

- ABILITIES

- BEHAVIOUR

- LESSON OR TOPIC OR CONCEPT

- TEACHING AND

- LEARNING

All the above are lacking. It is focused only on the SUBJECT OR TEACHER.

There is no participation from the CHILD.

ABILITIES of a child are not used, developed or encouraged.

Positive, constructive and mindful BEHAVIOUR is not allowed to blossom.

Passive participation of children will only enhance one sided treatment of the SUBJECT, TOPIC OR CONCEPT by the teacher.

The linkage or association between these factors is entirely and absolutely missing.

How do we bring in this linkage or association or bonding?

What is the solution?

Perhaps the best solution is to bring back the focus on the child and thus, make teaching and learning process child-centered.

Child centered: Teaching and learning revolves round the child.

The question that arises is:

- What is a child centred teaching?

The answer is that, it is actually a *'child participative'* teaching.

The simple way to interpret this is the fact that all our teaching should be focussed on the child. As the lesson is being taught, teacher not only teaches but also should be able to grasp a child's ability to imbibe the imparting of her knowledge. If this is not achieved, then the purpose of teaching is not served.

Creation of an environment, use of the appropriate techniques and deeply understanding a child's needs in being free from inhibitions are essential for successful teaching. The child remains the important focal point. The first step is the preparation of a child to listen and participate. To guide a child, a teacher needs to observe and asses his or her needs and requirements. If that is done, the next step is for the teacher to identify an appropriate methodology of teaching. Here comes the innovative ways to be used in teaching.

The amalgamation of opposite factors suitable to the group of students to be taught is imperative in an inclusive technique of teaching. A child is a learner. A teacher is a guide. If a teacher limits the teaching part to just being a helper to conduct or facilitate the learning process, this will enable a child to learn much better. We must remember that 'I DO, I LEARN' should be an underlining factor in the teaching/learning paradigm.

First and foremost is the level of teachers' knowledge of the subject. The primary requirement of a teacher is the mastery that he or she has on a particular concept. This is followed by successful interpretation of the knowledge. Teacher's innovation should be at its peak while preparing a lesson plan and use of relevant technique for a particular concept should be done while keeping in mind, the kind of group and the level of children or students.

Now what is the technique or style or method used for this concept at this level? Here lies the significance of methodology or pedagogy in imparting education.

Therefore child centred education involves the following aspects.

- TEACHER
- LESSON
- LEARNING
- CONCERN
- OBSERVES AND GUIDES
- PERSONAL TOUCH
- LEVELS OF ABILITIES
- DEVELOPMENT

<u>WHAT IS CHILD CENTRED EDUCATION?</u>

- A sort of revolt against subject-centred education

- The teacher is an interested observer and guide who encourages, advises and stimulates the child.

- Immediate purpose and interests are motivating factors.

- Modern education is child centered.

- Great philosophers and educationists like Rousseau, Tagore, Froebel, Pestalozzi and Montess have been strong vocal advocates of child-centred education.

It is believed that child centred teaching and learning is a sort of revolt against subject-centred education. Teacher is a guide who helps, guides, encourages, advises and stimulates a child to learn. In this process it is very essential for the teacher to know the child and his or her traits thoroughly before taking the step to educate the child. Each child's personal background, mental constitution, and their ability to understand differs from one another. A teacher needs to acknowledge the pros and cons of a child's ability in relation to the topic or the subject being taught. That is where child's interests become motivating factors and drives the immediate purpose of the process of teaching and learning. Today's education is essentially child centred. The emphasis on child centred learning is expressed by the great masters and educationists like Rousseau, Tagore, Froebel, Pestalozzi and Montessori at different times in history.

WHY IS IT NEEDED?

- I HEAR, I FORGET.

- I SEE, I REMEMBER.

- I DO, I LEARN.

- Let the child do and learn.

- Let the child act and learn.

- Let the child think and learn.

- Let the child play and learn.

- Let the child search and learn.

- Let the child read and learn.

- Let the child learn and a teacher only helps.

Now the main point that needs to be ironed out is the answer to WHY CHILD CENTEREC EDUCATION? In simple words, it means that the child is the learner and the learning that happens to the child has to be facilitated by the teacher. Basically learning happens by hearing, by seeing, by observing etc. But the wholesome learning happens only when the learning process is completely followed.

And this is **I DO, I LEARN.**

It has so many directions to be provided to the child.

- **LET THE CHILD DO AND LEARN.**

- **LET THE CHILD ACT AND LEARN.**

- **LET THE CHILD THINK AND LEARN.**

- **LET THE CHILD PLAY AND LEARN.**

- **LET THE CHILD READ AND LEARN.**

- **LET THE CHILD SEARCH AND LEARN.**

- **LET THE CHILD LEARN, TEACHER ONLY HELPS.**

So how do we go about this procedure?

- Freedom should be granted to the child to discover things.

- Develop plays, games and songs and occupations, designed especially to stimulate the child's self-activity.

- The child progresses at its own speed in a subject. The role of the teacher is to understand the child.

- The education of child depends on his interest and needs. The physical, social, emotional, moral and spiritual development of the child is "the main objective" of the child-centred Education.

- The main objective of child centred Education is to enable the child to learn through experience which is permanent. The course and subjects should be experience- oriented to meet the need of the child.

How can the procedure be practically followed?

- Freedom should be granted to the child to discover things. The more the child is independent and stress free, the higher the chances that her mind is without blocks and thus, is in a condition to absorb. This is where maximum learning happens.

- Develop plays, games and songs and occupations, designed especially to stimulate the child's self-activity. Ready-made games and songs from the market do help the learning of the child but uniqueness of teaching and learning is lost. Charts, displays, models, games and songs prepared with innovative abilities of teachers of the same school, is practically more useful in the learning process.

- The child progresses at her own speed on a subject. The role of the teacher is to understand the child. Instruments of teaching should be based on the needs of the child at various levels. These instruments are to be developed by relevant teachers at different levels of pre-primary, primary, middle and high school. These would bring in the required ways of teaching for students, making it not only subject specific but also student specific in a comprehensive manner. It would be better if it also reflects the requirements of society's educational system to cope up in a wider sense. Instruments of teaching and learning would become the strongest motivational factors by attracting the students and create interest in them.

The education of child depends on his interest and needs. The physical, social, emotional, moral and spiritual development of the child is "the main objective" of the child-centred education.

The main objective of child-centred education is to enable the child to learn through experience leading to permanent learning. The course and subjects should be experience-oriented so to meet the needs of the child.

BENEFITS TO A CHILD:

- Personalisation: Individual attention is given to each child.
- The child is *facilitated* and not taught.
- Every child is treated as unique and special.
- Leads to lifelong learning.
- The child is taught with a difference.

Why Personalisation?

As we all know each unit of creation in this cosmos is unique. We human beings are no exceptions. Every child is a result of various combinations and permutations. Therefore,the level of learning differs in each child. That is where personalisation gains its importance in teaching.

- Where the child is **facilitated** and not taught.

The right word here is not teaching but facilitating. What is the difference? Teaching is at one go whatever one teaches. But learning by a child is at various levels which can only be identified by the concerned teacher who is constantly in touch and is interacting with the child. That is where he/she needs to help, in other words facilitate a child, irrespective of her ability, intelligence, memory, expression etc.

- Where every child is treated as **unique and special**.

Every child is unique and special. I had a chance to experiment with this mode of teaching where each child is handled as per her ability and requirement. Though in theory it is very ideal, practically it is not easy but not impossible.

- There is no teaching. A concept is given as homework to be learnt.

- The child needs to read, find meanings, understand, pen down points of difficulties and underline those which are not understood.

- The outcome: Only a miniscule percentage of students went ahead and were able to explain the concept to the class, that too with a bit of hand holding.

- There were quite a few who tried and were successful after discussion.

- Majority were not able get the concept and were only able to absorb in pieces which led to a lot of confusion. It was very difficult to make them understand completely but then a child comes to you with the right attitude and tries to the best of her ability.

- I did find quite a few who were completely blank and there was no effort from their side.

- This experiment gave me a lot of insight into the psyche of children. Pragmatically to me, it was difficult to continue with constraints of time with the pressure of a heavy and elaborate syllabus to be completed. How do we handle students with such varied levels of intelligence, understanding and memory? It requires a lot of patience, control over yourself in every way to handle those below average students. In spite of all these idealistic means of handling children, we don't feel succesful.

This can be handled with a handful of students under each teacher given the kind of attention they need. But if this is taken up, is it commercially viable? Nobility of being a teacher takes a hard beating here.

- Where the child will not only learn but become a **<u>lifelong learner.</u>**

Let me announce that, which is well known. the fact that a school is not only the platform for learning but life itself. School is a huge stage where learning takes place with the successful handling of failures, exceptions being very miniscule. School is a base where this lesson is learnt with hard feelings without the anchor of a mother's lap. The child learns endurance and perseverance, to rise every time he/she falls. This is the best learning that a child takes away from her school which makes her a lifelong learner.

- Where a child is taught with a **difference**.

New technique, fresh environment, innovative methods, inclusive, inspiring, caring, understanding and secure attitude works wonders with a child. Gaining the trust of a child takes her learning to greater heights. Novel methods that bring the child closer to nature makes her a lifelong learner. This is what needs to be achieved by a teacher, teaching with a difference.

CONCLUSION:

- **Child is the centre of the whole education process.**
- **The great philosophers at different times emphasized on it.**
- **The role of teacher is like a guide and observer to provide complete freedom to the child to grow naturally.**
- **Child-centred Education is the ideal system to manifest the latent talent of the child.**
- **In this process education is not an extra venous imposition but natural stimulation for development of the child.**

The main theme is that the child is the centre of the whole education process.

- *What is being aimed at?*
- Complete education system is aimed at educating a **child.**
- *Why is it being done?*

- For improved perception and enhancement of the area of knowledge of a **child.**

- How is it being done?

- By making it easier for the **child** to learn, understand and express at various levels of child's intelligence and memory. Giving a learning opportunity and freedom for all levels of children with a secure feeling and atmosphere provided by the teachers and the institution.

- Great philosophers at different times have emphasized on it. Modern times have come to the terms and have accepted it. In today's world, this is being implemented as the only way for an easy and enhanced learning of the child. The other side of the coin is that the teacher is responsible for results of improvement based on the traits and characteristics of a child.

- The role of teacher is that of a guide and observer to provide complete freedom so the child can grow naturally. Hidden in this, is the unconditional responsibility of a teacher to see that this is systematically followed.

- Child-centred education is the ideal system to manifest the latent talent of the child.

- Educational psychology cannot be ignored as it is the crux of teaching and learning.

Ref :Wikipedia

EDUCATIONAL PSYCHOLOGY:

Teacher is the whole and sole for a student's learning. He or she is the singular or the only point of contact for education. In other words, teacher is a philosopher and guide rolled into one. The responsibility of bringing up a student and changing her into a complete human being, rests with the teacher. He is accountable and student depends fully on the teacher. It is the teacher's duty to see that the ultimate product of a student is complete with physical, mental, emotional and spiritual development along with an overflowing spirit of nationalism. Therefore, the role and importance of Educational Psychology for Teachers is very crucial.

Now what is this educational psychology?

Simple way of interpreting it is that every child is unique and special, has different physical and mental abilities and learns at different speed and pace. It is the teacher's responsibility and duty to teach every child as per their ability and pace and see that learning happens accordingly.

A teacher who knows about educational psychology, is aware of a child's abilities. He or she is aware of how to facilitate the child so to help the child grow into a beautiful human being with comprehensively developed personality. Thus, they can solve student problems effectively.

Educational psychology is based on the research work carried out by professionals.

This research process involves applying their teaching and learning theories of human development and growth to understand how they can be used. They work with people who are gifted and also with people who are differentially abled. It is very essential to work with their skills as schools are targeting assured academic success.

Educational psychology is a crucial tool for teachers to create and maintain socio-emotional atmosphere which is favourable and helpful in the classroom. As a consequence, the process of learning is effective in classrooms. Teaching methods are significant and are dependent on the children's progress. These researchers work and study children of all ages and use their analyses to recognize and categorize how their social and behavioural issues obstruct, hinder or hamper their learning. Now this has not only diversified to include preschool and higher classes but also spread out to adult educational set ups. These psychologists work with local authorities, families and others to help children develop into their full potential by identifying possible hindrances.

So the primary goals of psychology are to illustrate, elucidate, give details, forecast, foresee and change behavior. Some other methods are introspection, scrutiny, study, experiment, case study, meeting, dialogue, discussion and other methods. Any education in itself is a system which involves the process of teaching and learning. This should be sensitive to the changing environment and social changes which in turn will have an impact on instruction, assessment, curriculum, literacy, culture etc.

We say each child is unique because her characteristics differ based on talent, aptitudes, capacity to face or to defy, growth and maturity. These qualities develop into intelligence, originality, resourcefulness, inspiration and drive. On the whole, the educational psychology is the study and also its application. Here the teachers need to plan, implement and deliver with an appropriate medium of teaching to achieve the goal of learning objectives. It is the scientific study of human psychology to understand how it could be used for educational purpose. It includes the study of mental faculties like intelligence, memory and the effective way of using it the The scope of educational is vast. It is an unending process. It changes with changes in man's behaviour, societal developments, and also increase in the mental capacities and capabilities in the process of evolution.

There is an inherent difference between school psychologists and educational psychologists. School psychologists are limited to a narrow prospect and view whereas educational psychologists have a vast, immeasurable and enormous vision. This relates to adults or even differentially abled children. The former is micro, limited to teachers and learners. Later is macro, spreading its wings to the society as a whole.

Such is the importance of children's psychology, reiterate school psychologists and educational psychologists.

In this process, education is not an extraneous imposition but a natural stimulation for development of the child.

Progressive education emphasizes on **what to think** rather than on **how to think**. It should be more of discovery and self-learning where teachers are just facilitators. Child centric and progressive education essentially is the requirement of the day. A child should be ready as a citizen with life skills to face challenges of today's society. Just having a certificate having passed the examinations does not make sense. In today's world, you can even buy them. Education is not just that but development of knowledge and personality in the positive direction, which will not only help the individual but also society at large. Teaching should go beyond bookish knowledge. Effective changes in the curriculum and accordingly, horning of the comprehensive personality with knowledge, intelligence, skills and critical thinking appropriately aligned with the society is thus, indispensable.

Last but not least Parent-Teacher collaboration is the core for progressive education.

So, what is School Education?

Education has to be a beautiful journey where children enjoy, investigate, survey, explore, examine and study this beautiful world. It is not just class work, homework, tests and examinations. It is beyond all this narrow sense.

Education is a tri-polar process. The school needs to work in collaboration with teachers and parents. According to John Dewey, education is a tri-polar process. Any system of education which does not have a social significance, is incomplete.

He said, *"All education proceeds by the participation of the individual in the social consciousness of the race. Education is a three-dimensional process."*

<u>WHAT IS</u>
<u>CHILD CENTERED EDUCATION?</u>

If the child does not

learn the way I teach,

Then I teach the way

the child can learn.

SECTION – II
The Techniques and Accelerators

2.
LESSON PLANNING

Lesson planning is an essential part of educational system. Overall view of this is about how to divide the vast information available in nature for easy and simple assimilation for a child at different levels. For this, the information and knowledge of different subjects is graded at different levels of children beginning from play schools to universities. Each level is accumulated with knowledge, which is spread out through the year. Next is the responsibility of teachers to plan for the year at different levels.

This chapter is related to the systematic plan of the subject by the teacher for dividing it into yearly, semester, quarterly, monthly, weekly and daily plan.

- Grades or classes
- Subject..............
- Title or topic or concept
- Purpose or objective
- Tasks or methods or techniques

Lesson planning as the term denotes, is a systematic and organized technique through which the process of teaching a concept, a lesson or topic on a subject is divided into certain parts in relevance to its content and its divisions. In this context, we need to have comprehensive understanding of the whole lot of each subject to be taught throughout the year. This plan is further divided into time bound plans.

This is done for the convenience of the teacher, so he/she can teach in pieces rather than forcing the child to gulp down fully. Instead of forcibly pushing the entire syllabus down their throats but to ensure that they absorb it little by little so as to better understand and also express themselves in the process.

Now let's see how this can be done practically.

What is a Lesson Plan?

A lesson plan is a systematically organized lesson or topic a teacher prepares to teach his/her students in the class.

A lesson plan is a step by step preparation by the teacher either to make it easy for themselves to teach or to make it easy for the students to learn piece by piece.

A well-developed lesson plan reflects the interests and needs of students as well.

1. Yearly lesson plan

2. Half yearly or Semester wise plan

3. Quarterly or unit test wise plan

4. Monthly lesson plan

5. Weekly lesson plan

6. Daily lesson plan

Today's education system in general has grades or classes divided as per the subject to be covered in a year. This is based on the age of the child, their physical, mental, emotional, social and spiritual needs. This syllabus is selected by a chosen committee under different systems, like ICSE, (-Indian Certificate Of Secondary Education) CBSE (Central Board Of

Secondary Education) or STATE. Entire syllabus that is covered in a year needs to be systematically divided and organized in quarterly, monthly, weekly and daily plans.

YEARLY PLAN is a comprehensive, wide ranging and all-inclusive plan for a whole year to be covered in the class for the applicable subject. To make it easy to plan as well as to teach, this yearly plan is further divided into Half -yearly or semester wise plan, which further breaks up into Quarterly or Unit test wise plan, Monthly, Weekly and Daily lesson plans. Thus, the planning covers comprehensively from macro to micro levels so as to make teaching an easy tool in the modern world education system.

This is further divided into Half- yearly or Semester wise plan which takes into consideration testing of all the aspects of all subjects. This will certainly not be a burden for a child as it has been prepared through the semester.

Quarterly or what we can call as Unit test wise plan, can be stretched to 3-4 Quarterly plans depending on the number of days available. This includes what needs to be done or the quantum of subject to be covered in every three months. Again, this has the same advantages as Semester wise plan because this has been repeatedly taught and tested in three months. Overall probability is that the learning happens widely across all levels of children without any exception.

Monthly, weekly and daily plans are very helpful for the teachers as they know how much is covered, what is to be covered and most importantly, how much is learnt by the children. These not only cover written but also oral tests, competitions, play way methods which can also be assessed. These assessments improve learning among students and also achieving a better performance. Below average children could be identified and given extra help, based on the needs of those specific individual child. As the syllabus covered is very less in these days, a child absorbs and is able to learn without much difficulty.

What is Purpose or Objective

Objective is to make the task of teaching easy and organized for the teaching and to provide information for learning of the child in a systematic way.

May be through Tasks or methods or techniques

<u>How to Plan a calendar?:</u>

- **Total number of days in a year –Number of holidays = Number of working days**

- We need to divide the actual lesson as per the number of classes. First and foremost we need to count the number of working days of the school in a year without including activity and sports days as these will not have subject wise teaching. Number of allotment of periods for a subject needs to be done as per the calculation.

- No. of lessons or topics or concepts in the syllabus.

- After deciding the number of classes, we keep an account of number of lessons, concepts or topics to be taught.

- Allotment of number of periods for each lesson depends on the length of the lesson.

We need to allot maximum number of periods to longer or difficult topics. Lesser number of periods to medium sized lessons and minimum number of periods to short or easy ones should be allotted.

Thus, a rough plan for all lessons is created. The ones where we are sure of the plan, we can fix the exact dates of beginning for each lesson or concept, fixing tests or exams at the end based on the time period.

<u>EXAMPLE:</u>

<u>The Lesson</u>

- Subject: English

- Grades: 8, 9

- Topic : National Corbett Park

- By Ruskin Bond

- No. of classes required: 4

<u>With</u>   **<u>PURPOSE, TARGET, OR GOALS</u>**

- LEARN THE LANGUAGE BY

- READING

- LISTENING

- SPEAKING

- WRITING

1. Students will identify and describe the park and notice all kinds of animals found in the park.

2. Students will discover and learn about the descriptions and narratives from the lesson and appreciate.

3. *Materials:* Computer and internet to have a virtual tour of the park and see the jungle and the animals.

<u>What all to be used:</u>

- Materials: Text book lesson

- Computers and Internet or any digital forms for reference.

- Promethean Flipchart: Classifying animals and plants, trees from the National Parks or any other sources.

- Writing short notes after seeing the jungle and the animals, birds, plants, trees and cooling water sources like any water bodies available.

<u>**JUNGLE BEAUTIES :**</u>

<u>**MAGNFICIENT BENGAL TIGERS (from pictures – eg. online collections of Corbett park, India)**</u>

Collect beautiful pictures of jungle beauties of tigers and display them. Children will certainly be attracted to them. Get prints of these pictures to beautify the classroom.

Pictures from online can be displayed on laptops and computers. This will motivate children to be involved in the lesson. This will be a great application of technology for educational purposes, mainly teaching and learning.

<u>**ELEPHANTS STROLLING (from pictures- eg. online collections of Corbett National Park, India or representative images etc from different sources)**</u>

Display of elephant pictures strolling in the forest will attract children and cultivate curiosity and interest in them. Apart from this, students of all IQ levels will be able to follow and understand the lesson and absorb the essence of it. Video can be displayed on computers and laptops in the classroom. Mother elephants with babies roaming around in the jungle will be a big source of interest, attracting the attention of the children. If the availability of a projector is not an issue in the institution, then it can be used as well, leading to better understanding of the lesson.

<u>**DEERS GRAZING (from pictures- online collections of Corbett park, India or representative images etc from other sources)**</u>

Herds of deer grazing in the jungle near water bodies will make an interesting observation and will provide an attractive option for motivating the students to be more involved. The teacher can provide an explanation for all these pictures and videos.

BEAUTIFUL PEACOCK (from pictures- online collections of Corbett park, India or any other such sources or even sketches available for free download)

Peacocks are wonderful and attractive birds that will easily attract the attention of children. The teacher can make the class more interesting and learning easy and enjoyable.

- **State Objectives for the day.**

    - Show National Corbett Park (Internet)

    - Start Flipchart on animals and birds. Have students take out their text book references. Students will add new definition, illustration and drawing of the different types of birds and animals as we watch the Flipchart.

    - During the Flipchart activity there are pages for guided practice. Students will also use the interactive board as they fill in the guided practice pages in writing notes.
    Ask **Question** to the class: What have they learnt after virtual tour of the park? Have students write answers on sticky notes.

    - **Explain task.** Students will create different questions on the lesson about what they would like to know. They will try to learn and be prepared to answer on their own at the end.

    - Close with descriptions of different aspects and characteristics of writer's views on the National Park.

An essential underlying activity that will be achieved during this period is that the children are learning visually, through sounds and hearing and even by observation, satisfying their curiosity through this type of exposure. This method caters to all types of students who learn in different ways depending on which aspects of their senses are developed. Once cognizance and understanding takes place in a systematic way so that the child is able to answer all questions relevant to the topic.

As this lesson is for the English subject, let's assess how much it has catered to the following objectives.

LISTENING: Children are listening to the teacher, conversations between Teacher, students and their friends, to the commentary on video (if available). In the process they become cognizant of new things and understand what is going on during the lesson being taught in a particular way.

READING: This objective is in the process when children are reading from picture or text book lesson. This develops child's reading skills by enhancing correct pronunciation and punctuation in reading which not only develops expression but also confidence.

WRITING: Writing skill is another essential feature of language which reflects in a child making notes in the class, working on assignments given as homework which indirectly increases the vocabulary. This also improves sentence construction which is grammatically proper and the use of right words at right time for appropriate expression of thoughts or ideas.

SPEAKING: Basically, speaking a language is learnt through exposure to the right kind of social structure. Educating it in a formal way is implemented in the classrooms. Speaking is an art in itself. Speaking is expressing thoughts and ideas in a manner others understand. Just like in writing, this requires knowledge of vocabulary to a large extent for appropriate construction of grammatically correct sentences. This objective is also attained just like other objectives.

FLOW CHART (TEACHING) :

Flow charting is a technology based on smart technique for organised and systematic way of teaching that makes for a simpler and easier way of teaching and learning for both teachers and students. This helps a teacher, teach in a step by step manner, that helps the student to learn and understand the concept easily.

WHAT IS THE TOPIC OR LESSON -

WITH WHAT PURPOSE OR OBJECTIVE -

WITH WHAT ACTION -

<u>TASK OR PRACTICAL DOING</u>

- QUESTIONS

- LEARNING

- ASSIGNMENT

- EVALUATION

<u>FEW TIPS :</u>

Let's summarize:

Incorporating state standards is mandatory and unavoidable. So we need to stick to it.

The teacher has to have a very clear objective in mind to develope a very clear cut, impressive and student friendly design of the lesson plan. It should be easily implemented by the teacher so that the objectives are achieved.

Activities should be based on the objectives that are set up for the lesson plan. Simple activities with the available resources, need to be created to make the lesson easily understood and assimilated by the children.

Both the lesson and materials required for planning should be used to supplement multiple ways to learn. Main activities may need to be supported by smaller side activities which would illustrate the intricacies or details much better in an easily understandable manner.

Choosing the best delivery method is the mantra. Delivery method in the form of lecturing, discussion, interaction, role play etc may be chosen as per the requirement of the lesson with the students directly participating in it.

For example, there was a long lesson on cricket for a high school section. Best part of it was that my knowledge about cricket was zero. Added to that, the lesson was full of cricket specific jargon of which I was blissfully ignorant. But I had to conduct a class with that lesson. I read the long lesson again and again and again. I could not make head or tail out of it as I did not know about the game and what was worse, that I did not want to know as my interest in it was nil. But I had no choice but to take that lesson. I went to the class and announced that today's lesson would be on cricket. I could notice a sudden surge of controlled energy from boys whereas mischievous smile from girls. I began by saying that my knowledge about cricket was absolutely nothing. Immediately boys started saying, we know. My whole plan was changed on the spot. As I read the lesson, each paragraph was demonstrated by mock playing in the class. Boys were so enthusiastic that the whole lesson with every stroke of ball was explained by demonstration. The classroom turned into a cricket pitch. Instead of me teaching the class, students taught me and that too very successfully.

a. **Determine your method of assessment;** Assessment can be in the form of discussions, talks, oral tests, quiz, written short answer test and long answer test as it suits the lesson and the teacher. Here the point is that a lesson should be successfully understood and assimilated by the students. Assessment is clearly the appraisal of students understanding of the lesson taught. It is in other words, a review. To be precise, the evaluation that we think is of the students' is an indirect estimation of the teacher's potential and capability in performance.

b. **Use a template for your lesson plan, if you choose to do so.** Here the teacher has vast options. One is to make your own template depending on your ability, creativity, needs of students and requirements of the topic.

Second option is to choose a template online that is closer to your imagination of making a lesson plan. This not only saves lot of time but also gives lot of ideas that can be adopted if you will.

Third option is a combination of these two that will fulfill your objectives of the lesson plan to achieve a successful interpretation in making both teaching and learning easier.

3.
CLASSROOM MANAGEMENT

<u>Classroom Management Strategies:</u>

Class room is a world in itself. It's a mini social set up with an objective of learning and getting educated. This group in the classroom has its own dynamics with relevance to its age. CLASSROOM MANAGEMENT is a complex subject. Dealing with it is even more complex. Apart from updated subject knowledge, it not only requires patience in handling a heterogeneous group, but also requires understanding each child with various types of behaviour coming with different kinds of background. That is where the problems occur and needs to be handled differently.

<u>Behvioural Management:</u>

There are students who think that they can do anything with their power and strength in the class. According to them, might is right. They try to dominate in the class. They do believe in their own rules and try to implement them. But due to fear, follow school discipline. They are scared of punishment.

These kind of children need to be dealt in a tricky manner, where their ego is not hurt, at the same time psyche is handled in a soft way so that the mind is prepared for learning. Percentage of such children is very minimal. But its effect is like a spoilt fish in a pond. They cannot be handled in a tough manner, if done it will bounce back. Best way to deal with this, is to be soft and pleasing, get them involve in class activities so that learning takes place. Once he realizes that he is being cared for, his negative behavior is reduced, bringing him into the main learning. To write and to talk about handling such students is easy but practical handling is difficult. It requires a lot of patience, understanding the psyche of the student concerned and working accordingly, to get positive results. At the same time, it is not impossible. This approach needs a show of affection, patience, understanding and a soft touch by the teacher to soften the child. This can be done. With experience of the teacher, more positive results can be achieved.

This calls for motivation at every level. Motivating a child with Rewards and Punishments seems to be one of the working ways. In today's world, Punishment is discarded. But motivating with reward, praises and bringing out the positive points of a child is very important and is workable in most of the cases. Punishment is replaced by Reward, rightly so. Surprisingly, it works with wonderful results. It gives a massive push to the confidence of the child and that is reflected in a child's learning. The teacher needs to be confident of handling such children. If the teacher is not very confident, then such children might try to take advantage of teachers. Rewards can be in the form verbal praises, written compliments, appreciation in the group or may be a *shabhashi*!!. These certainly work to a great extent.

Students functioning in this category are in a developmental stage and mentally ready to follow discipline. When the teacher tries to discipline them in a tender way, they understand and follow. Too much of assertion will probably backfire. They are happy when praised and are prepared to follow discipline in the class. Their hunger for appreciation should be catered to and they are the best of students. In the process of pleasing they behave better, are happy and prepared for learning. The obvious attitude is, I am the best in my behaviour if I am cared for, loved, praised and appreciated. Teachers have no option but to cater to their all round needs to get the best results and creating a learning atmosphere in the class.

This category of children try to understand other children. They don't want to be taken to task or insulted. They are prepared to be obedient, once they are ticked. They are students who are moderate in behaviour and are happy to do as told. They are more interested in pleasing both their teachers and parents. They try to maintain discipline in the class because they are told to do so. They neither dominate nor bully others in the class.

There are a few children in every class who are self disciplined and don't need any assertion, either from teachers or parents. They know what to do, when and how. We enjoy working with them as they are least troublesome. They understand easily and work with diligence perfectly and with minimal mistakes or no mistakes at all. You can leave these kids alone with a project and come back 20 or 30 minutes later and find them still on task. They behave because, in their mind, it is the right thing to do.

Be sure you have the attention of everyone in your classroom before you start your lesson. Don't attempt to teach over the chatter of students who are not paying attention.

In one of my experiences of teaching grade 11 which consisted of students in their late teenage years, of around 16-18 yrs. There were three students, close friends, attending my class. They would have a very energetic conversation, continuously talking among themselves throughout the period. None of my warnings had any effect. I tried to find out from other subject teachers about these students' behaviour in their classes. Feedback was yes, and that it was the same in every class. Strict instructions from the management were that the students should not be abused or taken to task in any way. One fine day, I ran out of patience and ticked them in the class, which did not go well with them. The matter spread outside the class. There were umpteen number of reactions from all, from all directions. I maintained my silence and did not react. That was the beginning of their positive behaviour which I completely ignored in the classroom, but praised in front of their friends. This worked wonders to the extent they apologised me on Facebook. I was really impressed. All three of them completed their education and were picked by multinational companies and are happily settled in their careers.

It may be true that first instruction is to let the students know what is going to be taught in the class on that day. It is totally the prerogative of the teacher in the class, what needs to be done to teach a particular class with the lesson or topic. What kinds of verbal, non-verbal cues or gestures to be used to manage the class, is totally teacher's choice or privilege. These can be directly explained. As long as the teacher teaches and learning happens, and until positive disciplined environment is maintained, there should be no issues about it.

What instruction has to be given at what level or grades is different at various levels and is at the discrimination of teachers. These direct instructions need to be decided differently at primary, middle and secondary levels.

My experience says that the best way to begin a class is by telling an anecdote, a happening, an incident or an experience that motivates the children to listen and then follow the normal process of teaching and learning. That may be your own day to day experiences of some brave act or compassion or comical incident etc. In fact the whole class waits to listen to them, out of curiosity.

Taking the job of managing the class has two sides. One is the regular class management and during written assignments or tests and examinations. Instructions given during regular classes and during special times like conducting written work are different. Behaviour in a regular class needs to be checked every now and then. Instructions given at the beginning of the class may not work. So gentle reminders need to be given so that discipline is contained.

Monitoring a class is another challenging part of a teacher. A teacher who effectively checks the class by going round, finding out if everyone has started writing or written their names, are on the right page. She also needs to check if the numbering of answers is rightly done, correctly labelled etc.

She should be in a position to help a child individually in solving little problems so that the child can write smoothly.

McDaniel tells us of a saying that goes "Values are caught, not taught." Teachers who are courteous, prompt, enthusiastic, in control, patient and organized provide examples for their students through their own behaviour.

Teachers who communicate with a stern attitude call for troubles. Students who see their teachers as models are confused and behave with a mixed understanding. As a result, their behaviour is not to the expectations of the school and teachers. A soft spoken teacher receives softened voices from students. That's how communication becomes soft and matured. That is why a soft voiced teacher is always appreciated. A quiet voice is always pleasant, delightful and always longed for. A lot of responsibility lies with the teacher for her/his value-based behaviour as that will impact the behaviour and the personality of the student ultimately. Therefore every moment the teacher should realise that her or his behaviour as a model is always exposed to the eyes of children.

Now the point is how the teacher communicates without uttering words in a class. These are called non-verbal cuing. Some flip light switches. Others use clickers, though I never did that. I am very much doubtful about its effectiveness. Facial expressions, body posture and hand signals work to some extent. It is very essential that these things should be taken care of. In my experience, teachers were identified with these cues by students in their peer circle. That tickled them so much that it would become a matter of enjoyment for them. Best thing is to let them know what you want to convey beforehand, so that time to use these cues would be minimal.

A classroom can be a warm cheery place. Students enjoy an environment that changes periodically. Study centres with pictures and colour invite enthusiasm for your subject. Young people like to know about you and your interests. Include personal items in your classroom. A family picture or a few items from a hobby or collection on your desk will trigger personal conversations with your students. As they get to know you better, you will see fewer problems with discipline.

Just as you may want to enrich your classroom, there are times when you may want to impoverish it as well. You may need a quiet corner with few distractions. Some students will get caught up in visual exploration. For them, the splash and the colour is a siren that pulls them off task. Let them get their work done first and then come back to explore and enjoy the rest of the room.

For such activities, we may divide the number of children into groups and give them specific tasks to enhance the ambience of the class with various interesting display of pictures or achievements. For many students, visual impact is more effective in understanding the concept or increasing their information about various happenings, goings-on or accomplishments.

It all depends on the teacher to make the environment more colourful, the ambience more impressive and acceptable. Same displays throughout the year brings in monotony. For a change, classrooms can be designed subject wise or lesson wise or concept wise charts and displays that not only makes the child learn but also enhance exposure for the learning.

An effective teacher will take care that the student is not rewarded for misbehaviour by becoming the focus of attention. He/she monitors the activity in their classroom, moving around the room. She anticipates problems before they occur. Her approach to a misbehaving student should be inconspicuous, so that others in the class are not distracted. While lecturing to her class, this teacher makes effective use of name-dropping. If she sees a student talking or is off task, she simply drops the youngster's name into her dialogue in a natural way. "And you see, David, we carry the one to the tens column." David hears his name and is drawn back on task. The rest of the class might not notice this subtlety.

Discipline should not be asserted. The ambience created should be such that instinctively the child should bring in discipline from within. Discipline asserted is traditional limit setting authoritarianism. This is high profile discipline. The teacher is the boss and no child has the right to interfere with the learning of any student. Clear rules are laid out and consistently enforced.

My take on this assertive discipline is otherwise. Creating a friendly atmosphere in the class and making yourself a friend is the best way to bring in discipline in the class. Students respect a teacher who is like a friend and gives a listening ear to the children. Student's interaction among themselves is acceptable as long as everything is going on in the right direction. Silent classes which do not promote interaction lose on many fronts. They are non learning classes where there is no give and take among children.

To further the above point, normally students are more comfortable with their friends with better IQ in clarifying their doubts than their teachers. They depend mostly on their friends to continue their work with corrections to complete it smoothly.

"I" messages like *"I want you to..." or "I need you to..." or "I expect you to..."* are normally used for minimal number of students who misbehave in the class. It should be explained instead. That single child understands and behaves accordingly and thus, will create a positive environment. This becomes all the more easier and smoother if children are made to understand why it should be so. 95% of students know that a bad fish spoils the pond. This should be taken care of, so that other children do not get influenced. Such behaviour is rare, so it is not really a matter of concern.

The teacher who makes good use of this technique will focus the child's attention first and foremost on the behaviour he wants, not on the misbehaviour.

When the class is going on, a teacher expects the children to behave and be at peace to listen and understand what is being taught. If that doesn't happen, then the effectiveness of teacher comes down. To maintain her level of effective teaching, she needs to give certain instructions before teaching begins. Like 'do not talk while I talk'. It becomes difficult to understand what is being taught. 'Your doubts can be clarified after I finish.' 'If there is noise and disturbance, I will have to stop teaching, which is not in good taste as no one benefits out it.'

This kind of disturbance and noise levels generates a lot of irritation and frustration. It upsets and discourages the teacher. I am sure most of us as teachers have experienced this kind of behaviour in the class. Unless the teacher is clear and audible to herself, it is difficult for the teacher to convey these feelings to the children to contain the noise. Only a few students are troublesome. If the teacher develops a good rapport with these few, it becomes easy as these children begin to love and respect her.

Always be positive yourself when you deal with children. Instead of 'NO' we need to use positive phrases like, be organised, be disciplined, follow classroom rules, be good friends and help each other, eating anything should be during recess or lunch time, move in queue, talk softly where no negative word is used. Children should understand that classroom rules are important and need to be followed. Best thing is to shower praise on a child individually. We know that every child has good qualities. It is just a matter of how we acknowledge, admire and commend them in the class that ensures that the child develops and builds up positive feelings towards the teacher. The ultimate impact is good and acceptable behaviour of students in the class.

A very comprehensive and sensible contribution in general is to approach the online resources that are available on various educational websites where one can create a platform for teachers, students and others to learn and put their own points for debate and discussion. One can just give and take.

New teachers in particular should have an open mind to various channels of communication like news papers, films, websites, journals, documentaries, radio etc. One can add the essence of these learning in your classrooms to enhance the subject specific matter. Though the teacher is focused on classroom management, these matter help in enhancing and contributing to the broader aspects to make teaching more interesting.

Our goal is to take this Shakespearian masterpiece and modernize the teaching of it through the use of news articles, non-fiction pieces, technology, and recent news events, all the while meeting the new Common Core State Standards 1, 2, 3, 4, 5, and 7 through our lessons, group and independent activities, writing assignments, quizzes, etc.

This is nothing but empowering educators to deliver.

4.
Teaching Techniques (pedagogy)

TEACHING METHODOLOGIES:

ANCIENT VEDIC METHOD

VEDIC METHOD practiced at Gurukul.

- Begin teaching at the age of 6, though it was quite flexible.

- Memorize vedic shastras till the age of 18.

- Be an expert in a particular area.

- Contemplate and discuss until the memorized knowledge is assimilated.

- Intellectual analysis follows.

A gurukul was a type of education system in ancient India with shishya living near or with the guru in the same house. The gurukulam system gained a new tradition. The teacher is called as Guru and students are called shishyas. In a gurukul, students living together are considered as equals, irrespective of their social standing. Preservation and spread of ancient culture was the aim of ancient education system. The chief aim was to unfold the spiritual and moral power of the individual during vedic period. The objectives of education were perfection of physical, mental and intellectual personality of the student.

The **Gurukul** was a type of school in ancient **education system**. The **gurukul system** is an ancient learning method. Gurukulam has existed since the vedic age. Their main motto is to develop the knowledge and they were highly focused on **education**. ... The students will gather there and learn vedas from their Guru.

The main features of Vedic education can be briefly enumerated as follows:

- Knowledge

- Alms of Education. ...

- (i) Emphasis upon Knowledge and Experience. ...

- (ii) Spirituality. ...

- (iii) Sublimation of Instincts. ...

- (iv) Fulfillment of Duty. ...

- (v) Growth of Character and Personality. ...

The Method of Education:

Vedic method refers to the ancient method of thousands of years in Gurukuls in India. The scope includes the study of Vedas and spirituality, leading to moksha or liberation other than various aspects of life, earth and cosmos. This in reality is comprehensive and complete knowledge. Education begins at the age of 6 when all the faculties of the mind are properly developed. From the age of 6 to 18, the emphasis is on memorizing of shastras on almost all areas of knowledge. If the student wants to specialize in a particular area and be an expert, he or she had a choice.

It is scientifically understood that development of intellect is at its peak at the age of 18. Therefore, shishyas were considered qualified to contemplate, discuss until the memorized knowledge is understood and assimilated. More original ideas would come up and be added to the knowledge itself.

The basic difference between gurukul and modern school is that the gurukul education consists entirely of Vedas, epics, literature and archery and the modern education includes a variety of subjects like Science, Maths, English etc. ... In general the whole society was responsible for the education of students.

MODERN METHOD

- **Begin teaching at play school at 2 ½ - 3 yrs.**
- **Keep on learning all the subjects simultaneously.**
- **Understand, assimilate and contemplate until the end of education as a youth.**
- **Specialize in an area at post-graduate or PhD level.**
- **Contemplation and intellectual analysis follows.**

A teaching method comprises of the principles and methods used for instruction.

Modern method of teaching can be bifurcated into:

1. Traditional Methods of Teaching
2. Modern Techniques of Teaching

TRADITIONAL METHODS OF TEACHING

- **class participation,**
- **demonstration,**
- **Reading and recitation,**
- **memorization, or**
- **combinations of these**

- Explaining, or lecturing,

- Demonstrating-examples or experiments.

- Collaborative discussions

- Learning by teaching

MODERN TECHNIQUES OF TEACHING

- Inquiry based learning.

- Experienced based learning.

- providing worksheets

- projects

- tours, trips and excursions

- event hosting (exhibitions)

- field work

- visits

- team work

- use of technology (computers)

But whatever be the method, make sure we achieve the following:

- Make it interesting.

- Let the students get hooked.

- Let them be grasped and involved.

- Inspire, guide and facilitate.

- Let them enjoy.

- Let them express in what they are good at.

- Let them learn with freedom.

- LET THEM *LEARN.*

The objective is to make the class feel that learning is interesting so that the children are hooked to the topic. They should grasp the lesson and get involved with the concept. We need to inspire them, guide them and facilitate them. They should enjoy and express themselves in whatever they are good at. Learning should be with complete freedom and no stress. The objective is to let them learn.

Class participation

- **Make an interesting discussion as you are the band master.**
- **See that each one participates.**
- **Respect and listen to each one's point.**
- **Don't stray, come back to the FOCUS.**
- **Make it playful but full of points.**
- **Points could be noted down on the black board.**
- **Ultimately learning should happen.**

Under traditional methods of teaching comes class participation, which is an essential part of teaching that involves every student, so that the teacher is not only sure of the child trying to learn but also contributes in the process. In this process, students can clear their doubts enhancing the clarity of understanding. The child learns to discuss, understand without any inhibitions. The confidence level of children also increases.

Demonstration

- **Arts Partners for inclusion in their classroom-based programs.**
- **An attempt to show what the possibilities are for fun art projects that don't cost much.**
- **Demonstrate with experiments, games, plays etc.**

- **Let the teacher demonstrate followed by the child.**

- **This is learning by observing and doing.**

Demonstration is another way of putting across the concept or topic as practical classes in science subjects; role plays etc in other subjects. Demonstrating helps in understanding the subject matter better compared to mere theoretical explanations. Apart from this, a teacher can demonstrate values by being a model for the children. So both these aspects of demonstration are equally important for children to appreciate, know, comprehend and be aware of teacher's teaching the topic.

Reading and Recitation

- **Recitation is an art in itself. It has become a forgotten practice.**

- **It is a practice of enrichment of language.**

- **It improves pronunciation and sensitivity to language.**

- **It also imbibes learning to the sensitivities of life.**

- **Listening to recitation with expression is enjoyable makes it easy to send across the message.**

Reading a lesson aloud has many benefits. Reading helps in pronunciation, punctuation and figuring out what is being read. Reading aloud in the class improves confidence and sheds inhibitions. Recitation of poems is an art which is naturally there in some individuals. But it can also be learnt in schools. That is where this art helps in pronunciation, punctuation and verbal expression.

Memorization

- **Memory is one of the important faculties of the mind.**

- It is very powerful during growing years of a child up to 14 years of age. (During Vedic period, this natural growing aspect was completely utilized.)

- Even today our examination system is based on this fact.

- But how much of this is valid in today's world is an issue of serious discussion.

- How can we use it to its full capacity along with other important faculties like intelligence, imagination, creativity etc.

Memory is a gift. Memorization can be improved with practice to some extent. But those who are short of memory power are at a disadvantage. Our examination system is based absolutely on memory. Those who are blessed with it pass out with flying colours. Others are left out as mediocre. That is sad.

Combination of the above:

- This may be a workable solution to some extent.

- The students would get variety of hues in the class with inclusiveness.

- Many children would contribute their developed faculties with a lot of enthusiasm in classrooms.

- How it can be done is totally a teacher's prerogative.

- She or he only knows the best and can contribute constructively.

Combination of class participation, demonstration, memory, reading, recitation, also parallel writing or written practice would be wonderful practice on the part of teachers in making a child learn the topic or a concept.

<u>**Explaining or Lecturing:**</u>

- **This is the most common and traditional way of teaching.**

- **Even if the teacher is able to control the class, how many are listening, how many are understanding is a matter to be known only after questioning or tests.**

- **This method works fast as teachers need less preparation for this.**

- **This method can be conveniently used where the number of students in the class is between 30 to 60, which is the most common figures today.**

- **The drawback is bonding with every child is humanly impossible for a teacher.**

- **This may hinder learning for many children.**

Explaining and lecturing is a very common practice of teaching in Traditional ways. This is like one way traffic. There is no way to find out if the child has understood or not. The teacher keeps on lecturing irrespective of the children's responses. Though brighter or above average and average IQ children are able to understand, below average children are at a disadvantage.

<u>**Demonstrating -**</u>

<u>Experiments or Examples:</u>

A very common method with science subjects in particular. Physics, Chemistry and Biology are nothing but experiments galore to understand concepts. Other subjects are no less, being full of examples to teach and learn topics, lessons, theories, perceptions, ideas etc. This is essentially LEARNING BY DOING.

<u>**Collaborative discussions:**</u>

- **What is Collaborative discussion?**

- **A discussion is within a group.**

- **Collaborative learning is a situation in which two or more people learn or attempt to learn something together.**

- **Collaborative discussion is among different groups or teams.**

- **The scope of discussion is beyond a group.**

Collaboration takes place on a broader scope where knowledge and information expands. More and more points are added. Thus, Collaborative learning is commonly illustrated when groups of students work together to search for understanding, meaning, or solutions or to create an artefact or product of their learning. This is basically learning in groups.

<u>**Learning by Teaching:**</u>

- **Learning by teaching is a very enjoyable method.**

- **A teacher in general happens to be the most knowledgeable person.**

- **The reason is you keep learning as you teach.**

- **When you teach, the knowledge is reinforced and the one who teaches tends to learn in the process.**

- **So, the best way to make children learn is to make a student who knows to teach the class.**

- **Peer learning is more effective and works faster, easier and is a sure shot way for below average children to learn from peers.**

Children communicate openly with their peers without hesitation compared to, with their teachers when they teach. Their inhibition obstructs them from opening up when teachers are at it. Children who are knowledgeable on a particular topic are asked to teach the class. In the process, not only do those who teach improve their own learning but also those who are being taught, are enlightened to a great extent.

INQUIRY BASED LEARNING:

- **This is a very effective method.**
- **Elicit about ten questions from the students what they want to know about the topic.**
- **Write on the black board.**
- **Choose your own way to teach the lesson.**
- **Once teaching the lesson is over ask students to answer the questions that they had written down.**
- **Hold a test to assess the learning after giving sufficient time to go through.**

Inquiry based learning is a technique where a set of questions is prepared by the teacher, of which the students are asked to answer whatever they know. This is followed by teaching the lesson or the topic or a concept using a particular method suitable to the subject and the topic. After it is completed, we come back to the set of questions and ask children to write the answers as they are aware of details of the topic. They will write the answers, correct if required, complete by using appropriate words.

EXPERIENCE BASED LEARNING:

- **In this method, questions are elicited after going through the practical aspect of learning. Eg. Lesson on 'Gardening'.**
- **Children are equipped to answer as they have done what is given in the lesson. This method is based on 'I DO, I LEARN'.**

- **All the following methods are based on this method.**

Experience based learning is based on the kind of experience they go through in learning a lesson. This may be an assignment, a project, a trip etc. Based on the particular experience, the matter collected is organized in a systematic way and could be in the form of a presentation.

Providing Worksheets:

- **This is one of the best methods for reinforcement for students.**

- **The more they practice on the worksheets, the more they learn.**

- **Teachers are supposed to prepare worksheets considering the topic, levels of children and levels of worksheets.**

- **One can have three levels of worksheets for average, above average and below average children.**

If any topic or concept requires reinforcement for students, providing worksheets to students is the most effective way for students. Teachers have to take extra effort to provide this, either from online or self created worksheets for student's requirement. With increased practice, students learn more and more. As mentioned earlier, worksheets should reflect the topic, levels of students and appropriateness. These worksheets should have three levels catering to average, below average and above average students. Then only will it be a full-fledged and complete worksheet.

Projects:

- **A student must be made to do at least 2 to 3 projects in a year.**

- **This is a wholesome learning.**

- **Teacher can be a facilitator and guide.**

- **A teacher should give guide lines before starting a project.**

- **Let the children use internet, printouts, magazine, news paper cuttings and reference books.**

Project is supposed to be a wholesome learning. A student must be assigned 2 to 3 projects every year. This should be a part of scheme of Annual lesson plan. Students need to be given an introduction to it. Students should be guided and helped on how to begin, continue and end. They should be given guidelines before they begin. Children should be asked to use all sorts of sources for referring and including the required points appropriately.

<u>Tours, Trips and Excursions:</u>

- **I love it, I am sure many of you also love it, why not? This is full of excitement.**

- **Children also love it. It is a natural form of learning.**

- **The excitement starts from the beginning.**

- **It lasts through and through.**

- **It ends with lowest energy levels and they want to go home.**

- **Learning happens indirectly at every stage.**

- **Let them make notes, write stories, draw and sketch, write lyrics, sing songs and express in the form of skits, plays and dances. THEY WILL DO SO HAPPILY AND WHOLE HEARTEDLY.**

This is a natural form of learning. Children love it and enjoy it too. The excitement is there from the beginning and continues till the end when they are exhausted without energy and want to go home. Learning here is happening indirectly. They may write notes and stories, draw and sketch, write lyrics, sing and express in the form of skits, plays and dances, through which they learn directly.

Event Hosting (Exhibitions):

- **Most common in all educational institutions.**
- **Normally it is taken as only Science Exhibitions.**
- **Add languages, History, Geography, Math, Environmental and Moral studies.**
- **Help them and the students will come out with outstanding ideas and breath taking expressions in whatever form they may be.**
- **Teachers also should contribute to their subjects in their own way.**
- **It will turn out to be a complete learning not only for students but also for teachers.**

This can be taken as the most common in all educational institutions. Learning this at the school level itself makes them prepared for careers like, say event management if they want to choose it later in life. The biggest event that is held every year in these institutions is the popular Science Exhibitions and Sports and Annual days. We can extend this to many other areas and children would love to participate and enjoy them. We can add languages, History, Geography, Math, Environmental and Moral studies. My experience says, just help the children and they will come out with outstanding ideas breath-taking expressions in whatever form they may be. It will be great if teachers also contribute in their own areas. This will not only be a complete learning for students but also teachers who learn by experience.

<u>Team Work and Leadership challenge:</u>

- **In a school classes are teams and teacher is the leader.**

- **Your leadership qualities are tested.**

- **How to go about it?**

- **Accept every child, make use of the qualities of every child. Be positive, praise and get the work done.**

- **Let the children learn qualities of co-operation, co-ordination and collaboration.**

- **These qualities can best be taught in a class.**

Teamwork and leadership is a real challenge for teachers as their leadership qualities are tested. This is because in a school, classes are teams and teacher is the leader. The question is, how to go about it? We need to accept every child as he or she is and make use of qualities of every child. Positive praise always brings in positivity in the class and it becomes easy to get the allotted work from children. In the process, children learn qualities of co-operation, co-ordination and collaboration. These qualities can best be taught in the class.

<u>Visits and Trips:</u>

- **Visits are relative to the levels of students.**

- **Visits to the gardens, zoos, museums, meeting VIPs (knowledgeable people)**

- **Visits to post offices, banks, industries, closely related to life skills could also be arranged and its mock models can be conducted in schools.**

- **Visits to orphanages, teaching children of lower strata of society, old age homes could be a very satisfying idea.**

Visits to gardens, zoos, museums, meeting VIPs or knowledgeable people work wonders in speeding up the process of learning. Visits to post offices, banks, industries are closely related to life skills and so could be arranged. Apart from this, as mentioned above, visits to orphanages, teaching children of lower strata of society, old age homes etc could also be very satisfying. But all these visits need to be categorised and are relative to the levels of students.

Field Work:

- **Field work should be directly related to the subject.**

- **Topics in every subject give a lot of ideas on what kind of field work could be chosen.**

- **The subject and specific levels in a subject could be easily decided by the concerned teacher.**

Fieldwork is essentially learning outside the class, on a specific field/ topic. Every topic has a lot of scope in every subject to systematically organise field trips. Subject and the levels in a subject needs to be decided by teachers.

Use of Technology (Computers):

- **The latest is the use of technology.**

- **The scope is infinite.**

- **Creativity could be let loose to any extent.**

- **Use any subject, any topic, any software, any idea to be translated into computer technology.**

- **Empower yourself with technology**

In today's world nothing works without technology. Educational area is not an exception. The educational institutions are going in for it with open arms. Here the scope is infinite where creativity can be let loose to a vast extent. This can be used for any subject, any topic, with any software applied to any idea that can be termed as computer technology. Therefore it is very essential for every teacher to empower oneself with technology.

Use of Technology (Subject specific)

- **Homework and Assignments (Computer or internet based)**

- **Projects (Presentations using word, excel or ppt)**

- **Life skills (Reports after learning could be prepared using technology)**

- **Constructive deviations (Art, music, painting, games etc could be learnt through computer and internet.)**

- **Tests and Examinations**

- **Evaluation (Tabular form, excel sheet etc can be used to base evaluation)**

- **Value based education (eg. Stories like Panchatantra or other stories can be presented in animated forms)**

- **Creativity in teaching (the scope of creativity in technology is unlimited to be used for teaching)**

We all believe that unless what is taught is learnt, teaching is nothing but waste. Whatever be the methods of teaching, ultimately the objective is to learn. In today's world, lecturing method has no takers as the learning through this method is minimal and is not accepted though it has not been fully eliminated. It is practiced throughout as a basic way of teaching. But awareness of teaching through demonstration, discussion, EBL and IBL has been getting popularized and are accepted as effective ways to teach and learn.

The best way to learn is to teach. This is more effective than discussion, demonstration. Our experience teaches us that first level is lecturing which is overtaken by discussion and demonstration and even these have been left behind by learning by teaching.

Though I agree with this to a great extent, my take on this is completely different. All methods irrespective of being traditional or modern have their own place in terms of importance, effectiveness and outcome. Method of teaching to be used depending on the concept or topic of the subject and the decision on the process of lesson plan, is completely the prerogative of the teacher. He/she decides on the method and the course of action, progression and development for a specific concept or lesson depending upon whether it is an Art or Science subject.

- **Lecture** - **10%**
- **Reading** - **20%**
- **Demonstration** - **30%**
- **Discussion** - **50%**
- **Practice doing** - **75%**
- **Teach others** - **90%**

Ref : www.teacherssofIndia.org

5.
USE OF TECHNOLOGY

INTEGRATION OF TECHNOLOGY:

- As an educator, one of your responsibilities is to prepare your students for a society where technology plays a dominant role.

- However, be prepared that the integration of technology into the teaching practice may raise more questions than it answers.

- Whether you are new to Information and Communication Technology (ICT) or simply interested in change, or perhaps reconsidering the current use of ICT in your classroom, we cannot deny the importance of technology in the field of education today.

WHY IS INTEGRATION CRUCIAL?

Economic rational : Knowledge of ICT is very crucial in the job market.

Social reasoning:

1. ICT has permeated through every level in our society today.

2. Students quickly learn, grow and adapt to ICT in today's society.

3. The ability to incorporate ICT became a priority in the professional realm.

Educational reasons:

4. ICT enhances and develops Literacy Skills.

5. Encourages inclusive and individualized learning.

<u>While the importance of ICT cannot be denied, the other side of the coin explores what it means to be imparting education without the aid of ICT.</u>

TEACHING & LEARNING WITHOUT ICT:

- **There are plenty of learning skills that have nothing to do with technology.**

- **People in the past have been educated thoroughly without ICT.**

- **ICT reduces teacher's workload but it is still easier to teach without ICT skills.**

Ref : A booklet developed by (UNESCO) titled ***"Using ICT to develop literacy' UNESCO:"*** <u>provides examples on how ICT can be used to develop literacy skills.</u>

WHY COMPUTER LITERACY?:

- Combination of audio and visual stimuli is more effective than visual stimuli alone

- Aids in enhancing vocabulary and sentence construction skills

- can improve information processing and memory.

- Computer assisted instruction may be valuable in improving the phonological awareness of children.

- Talking books have assisted children to improve their reading comprehension and decoding skills.

<u>Using computer programs, learners can work :</u>

- independently

- Flexibly

- Self-paced

- co-develop both oral and aural skills

- Ultimately, learn to read

Computers can **encourage** learners to **participate in literacy education** and can **motivate them to continue to learn,** there by **increasing rates of retention** of literacy students.

Since computers are able to provide users with <u>immediate feedback,</u>

- Learners of literacy can proceed more <u>quickly and effectively</u> than otherwise.

- Computers and multimedia computer programs provide • <u>advantage</u> over radio and television in that they enable:

    a) <u>interactive learning,</u>

    b) <u>trial and error,</u>

    c) <u>manipulation of text.</u>

Essential skills:

In the field of education, the most essential skills are the following:

- **Reading**

- **Writing**

Using a Test involves:

- **Use of computer**

- **Use of thought process**

- **Verbal communication**

- **Working in groups or teams**

- **Learning as a continuous process**

These skills are all supported by **HIGH TECHNOLOGY.**

How ICT can support students with each of these skills:

- **Both high technology and low technology solutions will be explored for each skill.**

- **High technology solutions will look at sophisticated electronic or computer based solutions.**

- **Low technology solutions are less expensive tools that are readily available.**

<u>READING:</u>

- Refers to reading material that is in the form of sentences or paragraphs.

- Generally involves reading notes, letters, memos, manuals, specifications, regulations, books, reports or journals.

- Includes forms and labels

- Magnification

- Line markers

- Line masking Colour contrast

- Scanning and reading software

- Tracking/highlighting text

- Text-to-speech capabilities

- Adjusting the speech rate

- Built-in dictionary and thesaurus

- Highlighter

<u>**WRITING:**</u>

- Mind mapping
- Brain storming
- Picture based word processor
- Speech to text software
- Get their ideas down where this would otherwise not be possible
- Write more fluently and can improve spelling, reading comprehension and word recognition
- Be significantly faster than writing or typing
- Use longer and more complex compositions with fewer grammatical errors as compared with other methods of written production
- See and review their dictation and use what is on the screen as a cue for remembering their thoughts
- Context and phonetic spell checker
- Grammar checker
- Text to speech capabilities
- Integrated dictionary

<u>**HIGH AND LOW TECHNOLOGY SOLUTIONS AVAILABLE:**</u>

<u>**ICT Could be used in teaching with technology in all the following areas*:**</u>

- Problem solving;
- Decision making;
- Critical thinking;
- Task planning and organizing;
- Significant use of memory;
- Finding information

* Reference: https://www.teachspeced.ca/node/2

The following is situation/ roleplay is an example of integration of technology and teaching.

WELCOME TO THE DEPARTMENT OF ENVIRONMENTAL SCIENCE

We are here to go on a journey to Mars powered by the Dept of Environmental Science.

Ref : Video by NASA for educational purpose. A Journey to Mars – ROVER. REPRESENTATIVE ONLY.

Eminent theoretical physicist Stephen Hawking says that aliens exist. To trace them is just a matter of time.

Let's try this first in our own solar system and then our neighbouring planet.

We are with the spacecraft to Mars which is called Rover.

ARE YOU ALL READY?

Fix up your astronaut's dress.

Nasa: Rover finds clue to Mar's Past and a suitable environment for life to sustain and flourish.

A rover is a space exploration vehicle designed to move across the surface of a planet or other astronomical body. Some rovers have been designed to transport members of a human spaceflight crew; others have been partially of fully autonomous robots. Rovers usually arrive at the planetary surface on a lander-style spacecraft.

Rovers have to withstand high levels of acceleration, high and low temperatures, pressure, dust, corrosion, cosmic rays, remaining functional without repair for a needed period of time.

Rovers which land on celestial bodies far from the Earth, such as the Mars Exploration Rovers, cannot be remotely controlled in real-time since the speed at which radio signals travel is far too slow for real time or near-real time communication. These rovers are thus capable of operating autonomously with little assistance from ground control as far as navigation and data acquisition are concerned, although they still require human input for identifying promising targets to drive to in the distance and determining how to position itself to maximize solar energy, if it depends on solar panels for power.

Mars pathfinder, Sojourner, Spirit and Opportunity travelled to Mars. Both Spirit and Opportunity have been operating on Mars since 2004. Opportunity had traversed 15 kms on the Martian surface.

Mars has lost most of its magnetic field about 4 billion years ago.

Mars possesses ice caps at both poles which mainly consist of water ice.

Mars current climatic conditions may be destabilising underground.

Individual and mountain ranges effect local and larger weather.

Martian atmosphere is thinner due to various reasons.

Saltating sand particles have been observed on the Spirit Rover.

Cyclonic storms have been detected by various probes and telescopes.

High and low pressure areas with pressure waves dominate the weather. Mars is dryer and colder than earth and dust raised by these winds tends to remain in the atmosphere. Cyclonic storms do occur here.

Clouds are formed around fine particles of dust.

Temperatures vary from 27degrees to – 143degrees C.

There are no seas on Mars.

The Martian climate is regulated by seasonal changes of the carbon dioxide ice caps, the movement of large amounts of dust by the atmosphere and exchange of water vapour between the surface and the atmosphere. One of the most dynamic weather patterns on mars is the generation dust storms that generally occur in the southern spring and summer. These storms can grow to encompass the whole planet. Understanding how these storms develop and grow is one goal of future climatic studies.

Students: <u>Send us your rocks!</u>

Mars scientists are asking students from around the world to help them understand the red planet. Send in a rock from your region of the world, and we will use a special tool like the one on the rover to tell you what it's made of.

SEND YOUR NAME TO MARS

This is your chance to go to Mars!

Fill in your information below and your name will be included with others on a microchip on the Mars Science Laboratory rover heading to Mars in 2011! Wow! That's really chance of a life time.

This above method of technology integration was found to be very interesting and the children focused on it with pin drop silence. In fact, they were thrilled to get into the mode of travelling to and on Mars. It was so experiential that we all felt that we were there.

Teachers can take a cue from the above to use innovative ways to make their teaching interesting with such out of box methods applied and exploited.

6.
PROJECTS IN SCHOOLS

Projects are very effective tool for teaching in schools. They make learning exceptionally interesting. They are the best motivating factors for children to collect information, pictures and go through relevant subject matter to be used for the project. Having concluded that learning by means of projects, let's see how informatively and extensively we can go about it in a systematic or methodical functioning. Let us begin to analyse and study its various aspects.

<u>INDIVIDUAL PROJECTS :</u>

- **An assignment or a project (topic) is given.**
- **A topic is chosen by the teacher and the child has to work on it.**
- **Bookish project is related to syllabus**
- **A practical project is related to real life**

Objectives are:

- **Learning**
- **Organizing**
- **Time management to meet dead line**

An Individual project is the project given to each child to individually own and drive to completion. The child can take the help of teacher, parents and even his or her peers for that matter. Projects can be related to the syllabus of a particular level or it can also be a topic related to life itself. Whatever the case may be, objectives have to be fulfilled. There has to be learning about the topic. The base line is "I do, I learn." Learning to organise or systematically present helps in being systematic in life later. Time management is the essential requirement in today's life. A child learns about it in early life which will help him or her so that life can be handled, so to complete the work on time, meet deadlines and value the virtue of punctuality.

WHAT IS THE USE OF IT?

- **To learn, learn and learn.**
- **About the topic.**
- **To know and get more information.**
- **To increase knowledge.**
- **To organize the matter systematically.**
- **To learn about time management, to meet the deadline.**
- **This learning is basic to life skills in future.**
- **And of course for Grades!**

This is for all intents and purposes, in order to learn, learn and learn. But learning for what? Learning is about the given topic. To learn to collect information on the topic and understand it, is the primary objective. Indirect result is to increase the knowledge and learning about organizing the matter in a systematic way. How to manage time and meet deadlines in future life,also is the primary purpose. All these learning are basic skills of life, handy and helpful.

HOW TO GO ABOUT IT?

The student is expected to do the following.

- **i. Collect information on the topic.**

- **ii. Refer books, Magazines, news papers, internet.**

- **iii. discuss with elders, teachers and knowledgeable people.**

- **iv. Collect relevant pictures and animated displays.**

- **v. Organize the whole material in a systematic manner to give a form to the project.**

The above points on 'HOW TO GO ABOUT IT' are guidelines to go about making a project. The children are supposed to collect information about the topic. He or she can get paper or magazine cuttings, can surf internet for information, refer books, can discuss with elders, teachers, parents, get ideas from siblings and peers etc. Subject matter from any other source is welcome to be added to the project. Collection and use of pictures add to the project by making it colorful and more attractive.

To conclude, organizing collected information, pictures and animated displays is very important to make the project easy to read, see and understand the project which is the ultimate result of learning.

<u>GROUP PROJECTS</u>

Meaning of group project.

- A **<u>"group project"</u>** means you'll be working with a few classmates for a day, several days, or longer on an assignment.

- **Why are group projects popular?**

- **What you can do to make sure your group project is fair, fun, and successful?**

Group projects are about doing a project in a group or as a team. This is more popular because it is a lot of fun working in groups. This also helps in learning from each other and usually are very successful.

<u>**WHAT IS THE PURPOSE OF A GROUP PROJECT?**</u>

- Group projects are great practice for high school, college, and real life, when you will probably have a job that requires working with others.

- group projects can be fun and they often allow you to do a bigger, more interesting project than you could individually.

- With group work, you can actually learn more in less time.

- Group projects also give you a chance to get to know kids you might not otherwise know or talk with.

- Group projects are also a great way to practice skills you're not so sure of.

- If you lead, you'll know your whole group is rooting for you!

- Learning is permanent as it makes a deep impression on student's mind that is carried on for life time.

- It teaches the student with orgaising the material collected and also to be organised in the group so that learning happens.

- Individual discipline and group discipline is emphasised and the learning here is held lifelong.

- Shy and Children with reserved tendency open up and help themselves in free communication, thus increasing inter personal relationship.

- This will certainly help in enhancing their learning and understanding.

WHAT METHODS TO FOLLOW FOR A GROUP PROJECT?

- group work is all about talking and meeting with each other in the group.

- Take a few minutes to chat.

- it can help to take a minute to think about your skills

- share your strengths and weaknesses.

- Create together as a group

- it's important to divide the work fairly and evenly

- Important roles to play during a meeting include:

- The starter makes suggestions and offers ideas.

- The asker asks members to share information or ideas on a topic.

- The peacemaker looks at opposing views and finds something useful in each of them, helping people work out differences.

- If problems arise, talk to your teacher. Learning to follow methods is a boon for a child to face such intercommunication skills in future. Therefore the method should involve communication in the group with a free attitude.

- The discussion needs to be friendly.

- Group members need to be patient and listen to others. Here listening skill is handy.

- It need not be a debate but give and take of ideas with due respect to each one in the group.

- Each one's contribution is equally important. He/she can put across ideas and explain why it needs to be accepted.

- This again is a part of life skill that makes a base for life ahead.

- Any difference of opinion can be sorted out amicably and that is a real way to go ahead to conduct a group project.

Guide lines:

- Project is an important means of learning.

- There should be 2 to 4 projects at every level of a school.

- It is an essential way of building life skills.

- Teachers need to be helpers, facilitators, guides holding the children by hand.

- The learning in doing a project is infinite.

- Therefore there is no excuse in not having projects as a form of learning.

7.
VISITS AND FIELD TRIPS

A group of people going to a particular place with students is called a Field Trip. We can divide this whole process of a field trip into three parts.

1. Preparation

2. Activities

3. Follow up Activities

Preparation

First part that is preparation applies both to teachers and students. This gives both parties a much needed break from their routine life. Teachers study the selected place and learning objectives before taking a decision. Their experience gives them a lot of outside classroom learning. Their interaction during a visit to places like Zoos and nature centres provide interactive displays which allow children to touch plants and animals.

Activities

Lectures, tours, worksheets, videos and demonstrations fall under activities during the trip. All this needs teacher's preparation and they have to be very well prepared, including back-up plans of activities etc. The impact of visual learning is such that students are motivated to learn through touch, feel and listening. This also helps them to make better sense of the in-classroom instructions. This also helps in gaining a better understanding of topics, tolerance and culture. This also becomes a means of exposure to the outside world.

Follow Up Activities

Then comes follow up activities after the return. These follow-up activities could be writing a report, a productive discussion, a role play, a power point presentation etc. Children are in a better position to write about it, discuss and talk confidently on the topic, feel thrilled in presenting it in any other expression. Best part is that they become tremendously confident about themselves irrespective of whatever level of individual ability they may have.

As per the educationists, research work is the domain of adult people who thirst for knowledge and is usually chosen as an area of specialization for higher studies post college. All these techniques of teaching are also used in research. Let me tell you that research is not only used at PhD level, but also in pre-primary too.

Wondering how this is used?

If that is research, then what is field work and what are the projects given to children at different levels? In these field work and projects, all required material is collected, information is accumulated and observed. They are studied in depth. Ultimately, the result or the report that is created or produced is nothing but the ultimate assessment of the project and brought to the notice of all, as research.

My take is that even a pre-primary child also is capable of working for research. Their observation is very sharp and covers all that they experience with their five senses. These children continuously question and that itself is a basic sign of finding novelty in everything that they come across.

Eg. Give an apple or any fruit to children of pre-primary.

Observe what all they say by looking at the fruit.

May be they might tell you the colour, size, shape, taste and what not. In the process they shout, scream and perhaps, act naughty. But as they enjoy, they are doing research work in their own fashion. Outcome is what they are uttering. *This* is research based activity.

Let's break down the details, in a simple easy to remember manner:

What are these visits and field work?

- Your visits, anywhere, is the process of accumulation of interest.

- If these visits are activity based, then this is termed as field work.

- They need to be organized with specific purpose and have to be objective based.

- These visits are organized trips.

- The field works are with a purpose and are subject specific.Field work brings in direct contact with the topic.

- The situation experienced on ground, is field work and therefore has its own special place in learning.

- Fields selected for the purpose differ from subject to subject and varies from topic to topic.

- Students are excited, interested and are away from monotonous ways of routine learning.

Why are these visits organized and conducted?

- The learning here is comprehensive, elaborate and full of relevant information.

- This is based on the **concept of I do, I learn.**

- The teacher is just a guide; rest of the learning is automatic for students.

- This caters to all levels of children irrespective of their intellectual and mental abilities.These visits motivate children to learn in an environment where the learning is one to one basis.

- This is out of classroom learning where the curiosity of learning on their own is satisfied.

- This encourages not only self learning but also peer learning under teacher's guidance.

- The learning happens in such simple way that the student understands the elaborate exposure without much help from anybody, though guidance is necessary.

How are these visits and field work conducted?

- Firstly, they need to be categorized: entertainment, scientific, industrial, historical etc.

- These can be subject-specific.

- They can be short or long depending on the objective and relevance.

- Learning happens for sure. The child becomes more confident and there is no doubt about it.

- The result is it goes a long way in understanding assimilation of the subject.

- It stays in your memory. It helps in accumulation of subject matter to be used for further study, research, writing articles and books.

- Students are exposed to practical aspect of the topic rather than theoretical explanations.This exposure will certainly make it easier for them to understand it better.

- Mischievous students take in more interest in learning as they enjoy going out than what is taught inside four walls.

- Below average children tend to invlove, understand and assimilate through peer learning. As a result they shed their inhibitions and learning takes place.

<u>Summary</u>

- **<u>The essence</u> of visits and Field Trips is to ensure that LEARNING happens.**

- **Learning happens at every level of student life, irrespective of mental and intellectual abilities.**

- **Learning is lifelong and a permanent process.**

- **Every activity is research based irrespective of the level of a child.**

SECTION – III
Beyond the Classroom

8.

"LIFE SKILLS"

Life skills have been defined as -

"the abilities for adaptive and positive behaviour that enable individuals to deal effectively with the demands and challenges of everyday life"

In simple words, it means that every human being should have abilities to face challenges in life for survival. They should adapt to the situations and circumstances that define their surroundings and be able to respond in a positive way so to help them meet and deal with the demands that they face up every day in life.

The two categories of Life Skills could be:

- Thinking skills
- Social skills.

Thinking skills are related to creativity. These are creative skills which a person uses as a life skill to make an earning. These skills are based on creativity and training.

Social skills are those skills where people get trained where they are trained in a particular area which helps them to earn their living by serving society. Here the bottom line is to acquire the skills through training.

Whatever the skill is, it is best to begin at student level and carry it forward through higher education. Then use these skills to get hold of technique for living or survival.

'Livelihood skills' or occupational/vocational skills refer to capabilities, resources and opportunities to pursue individual and household economic goals and relate to income

Thus, Life skills are distinct from livelihood skills.

These could be painting, singing, dancing and lots more. Thinking creatively is also based on finding a new way to express and working through research. Bottom line is to *think and do.* A livelihood skill includes both occupational and vocational skills referring to capabilities, resources and opportunities to pursue individual and household economic goals and is related to income generation. They can be doctors, engineers, teachers etc. They are based on getting educated, trained, acquiring the skills to work. They may be electrician, plumber, carpenter, mason etc.

Occupational/Vocational Skills

- **Mechanic**
- **Driving**
- **Tailoring**
- **Carpentry**
- **Masonry**
- **Teaching**
- **Cooking**
- **Embroidery**
- **Weaving**
- **Book keeping**

<u>**The Ten core Life Skills as laid down by WHO are:**</u>

1. Self-awareness

2. Empathy

3. Critical thinking

4. Creative thinking

5. Decision making

6. Problem Solving

7. Effective communication

8. Interpersonal relationship

9. Coping with stress

10. Coping with emotion.

Self-awareness:

- includes recognition of 'self', our character, our strengths and weaknesses, desires and dislikes.

- Developing self-awareness can help us to recognize when we are stressed or feel under pressure.

- It is often a prerequisite to effective communication and interpersonal relations, as well as for developing empathy with others.

Empathy:

- Empathy is the ability to imagine what life is like for another person.

- Without empathy, our communication with others will amount to one-way traffic.

- When we understand ourselves as well as others, we are better

prepared to communicate our needs and desires.

- **Empathy can help us to accept others, who may be very different from ourselves.**

Critical Thinking:

Critical thinking is an ability to analyze information and experiences in an objective manner.

Looking or focusing at something and having an ability to analyze given information elaborately is a gift, not everyone can do it. To be a critic of something in a positive way and to bring out points constructively is an ability in itself. While doing so, one experiences both subjectivity and objectivity. But experiencing it in an objective manner, helps in bringing out points that are critical for positive growth. This is about understanding such feedback broadmindedly and being acceptable of it.

Critical thinking can contribute to health by helping us to recognize and assess the factors that influence.

Also, be aware that critical thinking does work and impact us in a psychological way. For example, our attitudes, behaviour, values that are influenced by peer pressure and the media. Critical thinking brings us to a broader spectrum of our thinking. It takes us away from subjective sphere of attitudes and behaviour. It helps us in reaching out to a bigger and larger field of the topic. Our attitudes broaden, behaviour widens, values extend. This is what helps us come out of peer pressure and the media influence.

i. **attitudes**

ii. **behaviour,**

iii **values**

iv. **peer pressure**

v. **the media.**

Creative thinking:

Creative thinking is a novel way of seeing or doing things that is characteristic of four components –

- **fluency (generating new ideas),**

  Fluency is focused on bringing in ideas creatively. In other words, generating new ideas for a particular way or method of doing, or it could be for a particular event, book or any other such concept. After considering its practicality or plausibility, this new idea can be implemented to verify its success.

- **Flexibility (shifting perspective easily),**

  Flexibility is a very essential quality required to be able to be adjusted anywhere at any point of time. Suppleness or elasticity of thought or idea is very important. Consider sensible and intelligent inputs that needs to be incorporated, so to make shifting perspective easier.

- **Originality (conceiving of something new),**

  The acceptance is, the more the original the more it is creative. Creative means something original. Originality is born out of creativity. If the idea is original, it is creatively brought out. A creative thought or idea is original thought or idea. Therefore originality in creative thinking is conceiving of something new.

- **Elaboration (building on other ideas).**

  Elaboration is extension, explanation, expansion, amplification or embellishment, embossing or exaggeration. There is already an idea on which other ideas are built. Therefore elaboration is simply building on other ideas.

9.
SPOKEN ENGNLISH

POSITION OF ENGLISH LANGUAGE IN INDIA.

English, as we all know is a language of Britain which travelled along with British traders, who superseded all other European travellers of trade with their education and enterprising attitude, who wanted to establish themselves in the most prosperous countries of Asia. Britain not only succeeded in commercial gains but found Indian society full of superstitions, which could easily be dominated socially. Its main representative, East India Company, played a pivotal role in this to the extent that English as a language was introduced in schools. This was the potential turning point which nurtured the deeper roots of Indian society. Thus it was and still is, growing day by day to reach the position it is in today.

People prefer English as it not only serves as a link language between the various Indian states and people but also provides that bridge as a global language for all those professionals with high flying dreams of living successfully abroad. To achieve their goal, they need global acceptance and for this, they have to learn English. The country is going through a transitional phase of culture where people who are ambitious and desirous to prosper economically, would like to learn this language and imitate western culture at the cost of indigenous languages and their culture. As a consequence, the spread of education is growing so fast that even the rural population doesn't want to be left behind in this race of perfecting the English language. There is a widespread learning of English even in the rural areas. This positive sign is welcome but in the bargain, learning our own languages has slid down to be neglected throughout the length and breadth of our country. This is a sad state of affairs. Where is this going to lead us to? Coming generations may completely lose the touch, which may result in the death of our languages, and ultimately our culture. Now is the time for all the intellectuals of the country to come together and save our ancient culture and rich heritage. I feel that we should balance it out somewhere by accepting English and enriching our already existing rich culture. We should not allow our culture to fade away in the bright light of British domination in spite of having gained independence at least half a century ago.

At times, I do feel that this kind of fear is baseless. Considering the thousand years of our culture and civilization that is quite strong enough to accept the positive aspects and filter the negative influences and thus, become much stronger in the process. We were probably dominated by them as we were not united as one single unit, were involved in fights among ourselves and engulfed by our deep rooted superstitions. On the other hand, British gave back a strong union – our country – they gave us a common link language, eradicated many social evils like sati, and encouraged widow remarriages through regulations. We were enlightened through various means, erased the image of being like frog in the well.

English language has been serving as a window to the world for us. It has brought us quite a number of Nobel Prize winners in various disciplines like Rabindranath Tagore, C V Raman, and Amartya Sen etc. This language is also instrumental in having introduced innumerable intellectuals from India to the latest wonder i.e. Computers. People are not only contributing to the global prosperity but are coming back to their roots and trying their best to eradicate poverty here. I strongly feel that we must not only pursue English language and explore opportunities at our door step but also revere and work simultaneously towards pursuing and developing our own languages and culture with equal zeal and zest. Every language of our country has rich and varied literature, contributed by the local and regional intellectuals which cannot be ignored. It has to be valued, may be translated and even presented globally.

Man is naturally attracted towards economic prosperity and learning English in the present times certainly leads one to greener pastures. Instead of accepting the idea that this gives way to slow and steady death of our languages and culture, I would like to be optimistic about the further blossoming of our culture because there is such an ocean of knowledge in the Vedas (holy Hindu scriptures) that it simply cannot be ignored. Many areas of Vedas are explored by Pundits and revealed to the people not only locally, nationally but also globally. If we allow it to die, we will be at a tremendous loss. I think it should not and cannot happen. The West is hungry to know the deeper layers of Vedic knowledge. To know about it, not only regional languages but Sanskrit, mother of all Indian languages, is also very necessary.

In this present scenario, English stands as the essential medium of exchange of ideas, thus giving an impetus for progress. It not only provides challenges to compete and grow with various avenues for further development but also ensures economical and financial progress leading to prosperity. India, already a potentially powerful country in the Asian sub-continent, could even be one of the global super powers.

Innovation of computer and its fast development is one of the essential achievements of present times. Contribution of Indian brains to the computer world is incredible and indisputable. Indian brain is recognized as one of the finest. This could happen only because of the English language that is added as a strong medium of communication throughout the world.

<u>For classes 8th and above:</u>

<u>Vocabulary:</u>

This mainly consists of enrichment of vocabulary with learning of innumerable words, their uses and usages. Vocabulary learning is an essential part of any foreign language learning as the meanings of new words are very often emphasized, whether in books or in classrooms. It is also central to language teaching and is of paramount importance to a language learner.

A vocabulary is a set of familiar words within a person's language. A vocabulary, usually developed with age, serves as a useful and fundamental tool for communication and acquiring knowledge. Acquiring an extensive vocabulary is one of the largest challenges in learning a second language.

Vocabulary is critical to reading success for three reasons: Since comprehension is the ultimate goal of reading, you cannot overestimate the importance of vocabulary development. Words are the currency of communication. A robust vocabulary improves all areas of communication — listening, speaking, reading and writing. (from web pages)

Grammar:

Whatever one speaks, needs to be grammatically correct.

Grammar is important because it is the language that makes it possible for us to talk about language. Grammar names the types of words and word groups that make up sentences, not only in English but in any language. ... "People associate grammar with errors and correctness. Grammar skills are useful in every aspect of life from education to leadership, and social life to employment opportunities. ... Proper grammar is also essential for understanding English as a second language as well as for learning a new language, since all languages follow grammatical patterns. Communication is a learned skill, to express themselves well and successfully, people must learn how to communicate effectively. Grammar lays the groundwork for effective communication. Thus, Grammar is very important because it helps enhance accuracy.

<u>Tips to Improve Your Grammar Skills</u>

1. Read: Reading may be the number one way you can improve your grammar skills.

2. Get a grammar manual. It is useful to have a thorough reference book nearby that you can consult when writing.

3. Review the basics.

4. Practice.

5. Listen to others.

6. Proofread…out loud.

7. Write.

<u>Pronunciation:</u>

Pronunciation is the essential requirement of any language irrespective of its origin. With pronunciation comes right tone and diction. For that matter, Oxford dictionary gives us how to pronounce the words appropriately. "Pronunciation" refers to the way in which we make the sound of words. To pronounce words, we push air from our lungs up through our throat and vocal chords, through our mouth, past our tongue and out between our teeth and lips.

Correct pronunciation is a basis for efficient communication in English, as in any other language. Significance of pronunciation certainly is something to be emphasised in any language and English language is not an exception. Proper pronunciation can be defined as a reproduction of language sounds in such a way that the intended message is passed easily, and is properly understood by a fluent speaker of the language in question. It can also be said that good pronunciation is the one that native speakers do not notice.

Pronunciation is important because it makes your first impression. Many English learners ignore pronunciation. They can communicate in class, so they think they are good enough. They think that they communicate in English because they can communicate with their teacher and other students. Therefore it is important to learn accurate learning of the pronunciation of words. Also, you will sound more natural and learn to speak English quickly. It will help you listen to English better, because you will learn to identify and recognise the sounds that other people are making. Your confidence will grow, exponentially.

How to Improve Your English Pronunciation: 8 Tips to Talk

1. Learn to listen. ...
2. Notice how your mouth and lips move. ...
3. Pay attention to your tongue. ...
4. Break words down into sounds. ...
5. Add stress to sounds and words. ...
6. Use pronunciation podcasts and videos. ...
7. Record yourself. ...
8. Practice with a buddy.

<u>**Narration:**</u>

With the enrichment of vocabulary, specific knowledge of grammar, adorned with right pronunciation, narration in the language comes with ease and rightly so.

Activities:

1. 1.Dialogues
2. Monologues
3. Plays
4. Narration

5. Debates

6. Reading

7. Television

Dialogues:

Dialogue is a conversation between two individuals. This can be read and spoken in the form of live talks between two persons. One can teach them to speak with relevant emotions and expressions. This can be practiced in the presence of a teacher who can check for mistakes, does corrections and even lead to enjoyment with fun and learning. Dialogue is a form of interaction between characters. Dialogue creates and changes relationships between characters and can also advance the plot or story. Generally speaking, dialogue is the main form of interaction between the characters in a story.

Monologue, however, is different from dialogues in several ways.

Monologues:

Monologue is spoken by a single individual and this is one of the techniques of literary plays. One can enjoy byhearting these monologues and narrating with perfection by repeated reinforcements.

Monologue is a long speech given by a character in a story, movie, play, etc, or by a performer. The main difference between a monologue and a dialogue is that the first one is a speech performed by a single character, while the second one is a conversation between two or more characters. The monologue is a one-sided conversation in which a person addresses a specific audience.

Plays:

Play is a drama where a story or a happening is written with multi characters. The whole story is dramatised and displayed or presented for the audience on stage. It can also be written as literary expressions in the form of books. It can be enacted on the stage in different roles. One has to learn dialogues and by heart them. That is how plays are an important form of learning the language.

Narration:

What is narration? It is telling, describing, unfolding or relating an incident, a story, a happening, event, occurrence, episode etc. Narration or story telling is an art. The support of a perfect language enhances the beauty of narration. Great narratives also involves the audience or a reader. Narration is the act of telling a story, usually in some kind of organised order. Narration generally involves any kind of explaining or telling of something. It is usually used in reference to storytelling. But how does it help in learning a language? Simple, it requires one to learn needed vocabulary, appropriate words, and construction of grammatically correct sentences to express one's thoughts. That is when the narration takes its form. The better one's proficiency in language, the better is his confidence. Perfection or mastery over language allows students to exude good confidence and go ahead with their narration, with appropriate expressions.

Debates:

A debate is the exchange of ideas and thoughts between individuals or teams. This can be one of the means to express oneself spontaneously, for which the mastery and usage of the knowledge of language is very essential. This is best acquired by exposure to the language itself. Children who go to English Medium schools from younger age learn the language as a result of exposure. The purpose of debate is to express yourself and speak your heart on a given topic. And then you will get to hear the opposition in your reasoning. The art of debating teaches you to prove your point, even if you understand the contradiction. It tests your reasoning.

Debating can benefit your child in many ways - from improving speaking and listening skills to building self-esteem. Learning to debate could have many benefits for your primary-school child. .These could be skills like improved critical thinking. Also leading to better poise, speech delivery and public speaking skills. All of this can lead to increased retention of information learned by the students.

Reading:

Reading is a very effective tool of learning a language. It helps in picking up vocabulary, relevant meaning in the sentence, right use of words, usage of grammar. This assists in enabling a language student to extract grammatically correct sentences in a language. There was a time when we would read news papers that would help us in not only improving our general knowledge, but also the language. Sadly in today's world, TV is slowly killing the habit of reading. Majority of children are not interested in reading. By not reading, they are missing a very important area of life which cannot be compensated with anything else.

It is necessary for every parent and teacher to motivate children towards this habit by making them understand the importance of reading. Elders can read from books, tell stories and stimulate, inspire and encourage children to read books at every level of their age.

Television:

Exposure is the Mantra.

My suggestion rather than advice to the parents and teachers, is to allow children to watch TV with age relevant programmes under supervision. Latest media of language is television. Just exposure to TV is enough to learn the content as well as vocabulary, grammar use and usage, pronunciation. It is like a comprehensive language and a general knowledge teacher for children. It is advisable for parents to allow children to watch their interest under their guidance. This will certainly help children.

Conclusion:

Key words are EXPOSURE, REINFORCEMENT and GUIDANCE. Exposure is providing the right kind of environment where a student learns with a free mind and joyful atmosphere.

Reinforcement is learning with repetitions in which improvement is shown or revealed until one reaches near perfection in articulation of his or her thoughts.

During the whole of this exercise, one necessary element is that of proper guidance. A teacher to guide the student is very essential to take the student on the right path to reach his destination.

Ref: From web pages

10.
CREATIVITY IN TEACHING

- What is Creativity?

- Creativity is something which has originality in thinking and implementation of its ideas in action.

In simple words, it is a logical and disciplined process of rationalizing, evaluating, analyzing the given information or a situation. Examples of creative thinking skills could be problem solving, writing, imaginary or visual art, communication skills, open mindedness. It is an invaluable skill that brings in new and freshness against old or traditional ways. Benefits of creativity are excellent team building and team work, increased engagement and interaction, improved ability to attract attention, increased fun, happiness and sense of achievement.

Some ways to enhance creativity is to take in challenges for new approach, new things, new thoughts, new ways of tackling problems etc.

- To understand the problem or a situation with open mindedness.

- To look at it analytically.

- Something which no one has thought.

- Start with notebook ideas.

- Explore new ideas with resources.

- Research other makers during class.

- Introduce mindfulness as creativity tool.

- Listen to fun stories to design.

- Brainstorm solutions to common challenge.

- Have a time bound project for creativity.

<u>Creative thinking is a new way or out of box thinking. It is looking at the same problem with a different perspective.</u>

<u>Creative thinking is a novel way of seeing or doing things that is characteristic of four components –</u>

<u>Fluency (generating new ideas).</u>

- **Capture ideas when they come.**

- **Think macro.**

- **Speak and share your ideas.**

- **Ask more questions.**

- **Focus on ideas that solve problems.**

- **Apply same ideas on opposite views.**

- **Make things as simple as possible for children and students.**

It is capturing ideas or thoughts whenever they strike and preferably note it down. Collect such ideas, collate with other's thoughts, add information or appropriate data to it. Add opinions, feelings, attitude to emboss your idea into a new creative initiative or design. Let your thought be macro. It should be broad and comprehensive. It need not be a small or a narrow view. Sharing will bring in newer concepts to the creativity. Speak about it and exchange thoughts to improve and enlarge your creative ways. More questions give more methods of solving problems which would enhance creative angles to teaching. Focus on scheme or plan on solving problems. Try same ways on opposite proposals and initiatives. Ultimately the intention is to make it as simple and easy as possible for children and students to learn.

Flexibility (shifting perspective easily).

- **Innovation is bringing in something new.**
- **Be prepared for the change or the shift.**
- **Welcome new changes.**
- **Being flexible is the mantra.**
- **Human mind tends to refuse change.**
- **We need to change it.**

Flexibility refers to the abililty to change easily. This could be elasticity, suppleness, softness or even that which can be stretched or shaped easily. All of this is an integral part of creativity. This is also helpful in shifting perspectives easily. This is a new thought, an innovative idea that brings in something new. There is a need to be prepared for the change or shift. This brings with it changes which are welcome, new changes which are to be accepted with open arms as they are good for the process of teaching that will help not only teachers but also students and parents and ultimately the society. In short, being flexible is the mantra. Flexibility is stretchable and is inclusive. All inclusive innovative ideas should essentially be simple and easily implemented. Human mind gets habituated and refuses to change. We need to welcome change for the betterment of teachers, students and parent communities.

Originality (conceiving of something new).

- **Originality is thinking and doing something beyond whatever is available.**
- **Bringing in freshness of ideas and innovative acts.**
- **It is something that is raw in structure which needs to be worked**

out to be different than that is available.

- **Outcome of individual idea, team work or brain storming.**

What is originality? In simple terms it is innovation, novelty, uniqueness or inventiveness or creativity. Teachers need to use this quality in their teaching process. It brings in a fresh perspective for the teacher as well as the learner. This actually means conceiving something new. It is thinking and doing something beyond whatever is available. Teaching methods or means should bring in fresh ideas and innovative acts. This ensures that the teacher's creativity will motivate children with original ideas. A raw idea is worked out to change it into a unique technique, which will be transformed into a polished means or method of teaching that would interest children and motivate them to learn. This is very rarely done by individuals in the education sector. Though this is an outcome of an individual idea, team work and brainstorming will certainly work wonders to make it a brilliant method of teaching.

<u>Elaboration (building on other ideas).</u>

- **A thought, an idea or an original act can be elaborated in many ways.**

- **An idea can be built around by other ideas.**

- **A thought can be developed with wrapping in of others.**

- **A comprehensive and wide range of new concept can be created by explanation, expansion and amplification.**

In creativity, a simple but original thought can be added with other ideas. Other concepts can be woven around the idea. This can be elaborated in various directions. More relevant explanations could be given to develop these thoughts. Building around this creative idea would be lot of fun when working in a team including broader spectrum. Development of the thought could be covering wider area, working extensively by expanding it in more than one way. One can put in explanations for the idea. Expansion of the thought in different directions will bring in more design, plan or schemes of things to be wrapped up for further development of the idea. Creative thought can be amplified in unlimited ways by applying various innovative methods.

Conclusion

- **Every point and every step of growth in this cosmos is the result of varied and innumerable permutations and combinations.**

- **That is what we need to push ourselves to get into creativity individually, socially, nationally into learning and teaching.**

- **Therefore the need of the hour is to push creativity into learning and teaching across all levels individual, social or national.**

Eg. The following could be a lesson plan that incorporates creativity and innovation.

An Essay on "Compassion towards Animals and Birds""A refined and a compassionate approach towards ANIMALS, BIRDS AND NATURE"

What?

- Introduction

- What is compassion?

- What is compassion towards animals, birds and nature?

<u>**Why?**</u>

- Why should we be concerned about them?
- How do they impact us?
- The earth belongs to them too.
- Without them we lose out on the chain in nature.
- Nature consists not only humans and plants but animals and birds too.
- Therefore protection of our environment along with plants and animals is equally important.

<u>**How?**</u>

- Empathy towards environment.
- Treating birds and animals as we treat ourselves.
- Not to be cruel to them.
- Treat with compassion.
- Using animals and birds for experiments should be banned.
- Using them for medicinal purpose must be banned.
- Law against using them for entertainments and circus should be banned, if done should be legally and heavily penalized.
- Becoming a vegan which means a vegetarian will lead to not killing animals and birds for consuming.

<u>**Conclusion**</u>

All these and any other path of saving them with compassion should be taught, spread and make them understand among people and implement them with seriousness

<u>This can be a topic with creativity. Discuss and debate in the class with</u>

all these points (more points can be added)

Let them go to the extent of assimilation of these points sinking to the depth and write the composition in an organised and good English with appropriate vocabulary. Support them with the relevant words and expressions.

Help students to make a questionnaire on few points involving what, why and how.Let them take these questionnaire to family members, friends, teachers and any one who can contribute to the questionnaire.

Now organise the content of these answers which will help in forming content for the essay.

Now organise the content and as per teacher's guidelines and write.

This will be a sort of use of creativity by the teacher.

11.

VALUE- BASED TEACHING

Value based education demands that we need to provide a better place for our children in this world. And we as teachers are bound by this responsibility.

As long as we as teachers believe in the above and follow moral values, there won't be any dearth of moral values in our children. Once we as teachers follow them, it automatically gets inculcated into the children that we come into contact with.

What do we understand by Value Based Teaching?

Value based teaching is to ensure that children realise the values of life and implement them in their lives to bring in positive ambience in their own social environments. Thus enhancing the whole society morally and avoiding unnecessary disturbances that may cause harm to the society . Value based education inculcates positive and healthy habits for mental, psychological and emotional health of individuals in a society.This needs to be nurtured and developed from a young age among children.

Values are essential part of any social and family life. A value based society is organised and systematically placed as a part of our life. Without values, society will be in chaos. Values are at every level of life in a society. Individual values, social values, group values etc. Values are essential for smooth functioning of a family, society, school, educational institutions, business and industrial organisations etc.

Therefore, it is essential to inculcate this habit at a young age among children. That is where values-based education takes an important place in educational institutions like schools. A young mind is easily influenced by thoughts and acts. Picking up values in childhood is easier and life-long lasting.

Few values worth mentioning are:

- **Honesty**
- **Kindness**
- **Sympathy**
- **Empathy**
- **Respecting elders**
- **Politeness**
- **Caring**
- **Sharing**

<u>Why is this essential?</u>

Teaching moral values in schools starting from pre-primary is necessary. Learning moral values transforms a person into a complete human being. Therefore it needs to be taught at school levels so that they get deep rooted at an early phase of life. They make him/her a responsible person who understands and cares for others. Be it humans, animals or even plants. The complete nature and the whole cosmos. He/she respects everything around them and is empathetic to every single creation.

Value based education deals directly with teaching values. This can be worked either directly or indirectly which gets incorporated in their personality lifelong. This contributes to the well being of not only society and the country but also the whole of humanity.

This is one of the sure shot ways to transmit values to the next generation. Lack of values is an essential component which contributes to the ills of society like corruption, disrespect and abuse of women, increase in anti-social behaviors etc. Value based education supports strong bonding between student and teacher and this stays lifelong.

Need of the day is to introduce moral values as a part of syllabus in schools.

Few values like unconditional love and kindness, honesty, hard work, respect for others, co-operation, compassion and forgiveness need to be highlighted in the behavioural ways of children.

It is sad to see that values and their teaching is seen minimally in schools today. Therefore, we find so much of violence, dishonesty and bad influences in the society and this is increasing day by day. Further to this, the youth is getting easily trapped by these negativities in the society and the society and nation at large is thoroughly getting polluted. The base of the youth is so much shattered that they are out on the street and display violence which is unwelcome. This is due to lack of moral values. It is the duty of schools, teachers, elders and families to take care of values being ingrained in the personalities of youth which would in the long run, change the ambience of the whole nation. We as educators, are essentially responsible for the well being of the nation as the teachers of moral values.

How is it possible?

- **Telling stories**
- **Panchatantra Stories   (a comprehensive learning about values from India)**
- **Audio Visuals**
- **Grand ma tales (Selected funny ones with messages)**
- **Satsang on social platforms (Social Values)**
- **Family as unit of learning**
- **Values taught at school**

We had something called grand ma stories in our ancient ways of living in joint families which is missing in today's society. These stories were narrated to children in the family in a very interesting way. As a child's mind is very impressionable at young age, these value based stories have a permanent impact on children. Our society has lost this centuries old practice due to sprouting of nuclear families. We need to revive this for our children's sake, our sake and the society at large.

Panchatantra stories is the ancient literature of our civilization which is based on animals and plants and their behaviours, which in turn would be shared in families among children. They are universal and can be used even today which is rarely included in the western mode of education system. This has to be thought through very seriously. Efforts should be made to include this into the syllabus of all educational systems like ICSE, CBSE, State boards etc. Only then will there be positivity in the social environment.

In ancient times, lack of technology did not effect the teaching of such values. Puppet shows would influence children as effectively as any high-tech gadgets. Plays of Mahabharata and Ramayana in villages during festivals and melas would be a place of attraction to witness as audience which would certainly spread positive messages in the society. Today we have plays, films, songs, audio visuals for spreading constructive, affirmative, encouraging and upbeat messages. All these could be used to reach out to children or students in schools that would widen a children's mental faculties to develop value based set up in societies at large.

Satsangs in societies, grand ma tales, cherished values in the family passing on through generations, respect and recognising values in nuclear families, essential values taught in schools, go a long way in upholding these social values permanently.

To conclude, Value Based Learning is the requirement of the day at all school levels as an antidote for the violence, corruption, ill treatment of women at every strata of society, disrespect for elders, springing up of old age homes are few negativities of society which need to be curtailed. The only solution for all this is VALUE BASED TEACHING AND LEARNING IN SCHOOLS. This not only influences behaviour among students in society but also considering EARTH as a home, extending these values towards their attitude to the plant and animal kingdom. Our ancient wisdom teaches us to respect, and be empathetic and considerate towards Mother Earth, all living and non-living things and the cosmos at large. We as a unit are an extension of everything else in this creation.

The need of the hour is, for children, passing out of school to be imbibed with moral values and the feelings of nationalism. Else the whole purpose of education is null and void.

SECTION – IV
Measuring the Impact

12.
HOMEWORK

What is Homework?

- Homework refers to tasks assigned to students

- by their teachers to be completed

- outside of class.

<u>Objectives:</u>

- to increase knowledge

- improve abilities

- to enhance the skills of students.

Home work is the task assigned for student to be completed outside the class room. As the name itself suggests it is the work done or studied at home. Home work is given by the teachers based on the lesson completed in the class. Perhaps this is just to know how much has the child absorbed or understood that topic. Objective is to increase children's knowledge of the topic or concept that has been discussed or taught in the classroom. This also enhances and improves a child's abilities. In doing homework, the child works on his/her own or completes the same with the help of elders at home. This in turn develops, augments and improves the skills of the students.

In today's world, there are differing and opposite views and opinions on Homework. One is Pro-homework and the other is Anti-homework. Let's discuss each one. Let's begin with Pro-homework.

PRO HOMEWORK

- **It is a must.**

- **It helps reinforcement.**

- **Reinforcement or Repetition strengthens memory.**

- **The child is busy at home.**

- **Let the child complete the homework and then reward him or her.**

- **Are you done with the same?**

It means homework is so essential that it should be finished first.

Today's educationists carry two views on Homework. One set of teachers with conventional thoughts are pro-homework. They believe in giving homework to students as a part of regular teaching and learning. This school of thought feels that home work is very essential as it helps in learning by reinforcement. Reinforcement or repetition increases memory and is one of the components which necessarily help in the development of memory. The child is kept busy at home. Let the homework be done with. And then it is the rewarding time for her or him.

ANTI HOMEWORK

- **Children should not be burdened.**

- **They should be given free time at home.**

- **Creativity, play and free peer interaction should replace.**

- **Children should spend time positively in other ways of learning.**

Another school of thought recommends anti homework. The idea is that children should not be burdened. Learning should take place naturally without any burden or stress. The free mind is the best learning ground. Their time at home should not be used continuously for homework. They should be given free time at home to explore other aspects of life. Rightly so, creativity, play and free peer interaction should replace. Whatever learning happens, it should be at school. At home, children should spend time in other things than just homework. Time should necessarily be spent positively in other ways. In this way children learn happily what they want and can pursue what they are interested in. Through this learning happens freely, happily and is a sure shot for learning successfully

PRO HOMEWORK:

- **homework is a way to stay connected to their children's learning.**
- **It makes parents "nags, bribers, and taskmasters."**
- **two to four hours of homework at night**
- **plus weekend and vacation projects.**
- **He was overwhelmed and struggled to finish assignments.**
- **"Parents think it is strange when their children are not assigned a substantial amount of homework."**
- **"the concept of homework "has become so ingrained.**
- **commitment to the idea of homework exists strongly.**

Pro-homework thought appeases people because they believe that homework connects students and teacher's teaching. It makes parents nags as they are continuously after homework. Few parents are bribers motivating children to complete the work. Few parents are even task masters, which is a negative way to teach. But the truth is, that learning does not happen fully. Two to four hours of homework at night is actually too much for children. Added to it, weekend and vacation projects spoil the mood and an indirect way of learning through exploring does not happen, leaving the child's mental growth stunted. The reason is children are overwhelmed and struggle to finish assignments. The concept of homework is so ingrained to our idea of school learning that we cannot think of a school without homework. Commitment to the idea of homework exists so strongly that conventional idea of homework is the only thing that a school of parents and teachers are convinced about.

ANTI HOMEWORK:

- **The principal got rid of homework.**

- **Instead of teachers sending kids home with math worksheets and spelling flash cards,**

- **Students would instead go home and read.**

- **Every day for 30 minutes, or more**

- **if they had time or the inclination,**

- **with parents or on their own.**

- **not spend night after night doing rote homework drills.**

- **"mechanical homework," leads to conditions like childhood nervousness and eyestrain.**

- **homework is an intrusion on family life.**

- **states like California passed laws abolishing homework for students under a certain age.**

- **Students are stressed and miss out on family life.**

- **Already 6 to 9 hrs of work is spent during the day doing schoolwork.**

- **creates a tug-of-war between parents and children.**

Anti homework concept results in getting the homework being cancelled by the Principal. What a relief for all the teaching staff!! But we need to find out how much it helps or does not help in a practical way. There are no worksheets or spelling flash cards, no science work sheets or no objective questionnaires. Instead children have to go home and read on their own by recollecting classroom teaching and discussions and learn to understand the lesson or concept. This initiates the child to involve and try to learn. The question is how many can do this? How many are able to learn without any help at home? This leads to the question, is there any one to help at home when both parents go for work. Or the child has to depend on tuition teachers. Then the whole exercise of this concept will be futile. But this discourages night after night homework, of doing rote homework drills. These continuous mechanical drills would not only strain one's eyes but also leads to affected nervous conditions. Many would feel that children's homework is an intrusion on the family life. This was a continuous strain on family to come under the stress and nervous conditions, outcome of which was health issues including eye strain. In America, states like California have passed laws restricting homework under certain age conditions. As per the concept, students are so stressed that they miss family life. Already they spend 6 to 9 hours in schools and extending it to home also is very harsh on the part of society.

This creates friction, a sort of tug of war, bad relationship with parents which is not a welcome by any means.

<u>WHY HOMEWORK:</u>

- **Not everyone is convinced that homework as a given thing is a bad thing.**

- **It is helping them develop certain skills.**

- **It can foster positive character traits such as independence and responsibility.**

- **Homework can teach children how to manage time.**

- **Builds confidence in competition.**

- **In lower levels you'll just make them tired and cross.**

- **homework has to be relevant.**

- **To be in control of their academic futures, requires hard work, and homework is a part of it."**

Therefore it is very clearly understandable, apparent and obvious that everyone is not convinced that homework is a bad practice. According to many, it is helping them to develop skills, is a means or a method to reinforce and comprehend what they have been taught in schools.

Character traits of independence and responsibility are fostered in children, enhancing their personality growth. Again, time management is a part of children's learning which gets embedded in the early phase of life itself. Completing a given task irrespective of elderly or peer help builds confidence and prepares mentally for competition. Homework which works as reinforcement, will develop memory and retention power of the child. Home work has to be relevant which generally is and calculated, measured and level wise to avoid tiresomeness and fatigue for a child. Academic futures of children demand and require hard work, and homework is a part of it. It helps to be in control of their academic futures.

HOW SHOULD IT BE TAKEN UP?:

- **It should be decided level wise.**
- **How much work?**
- **How much time?**
- **How many subjects per day?**
- **A weekly time table could be made to include all subjects.**
- **On an average two subjects per day.**
- **Less time for lower levels and more time for higher levels.**
- **Time range could range from just 10 minutes to one and half or two hours.**

Homework should always be decided level wise. Homework measured, suitable, appropriate, and relevant to classroom teaching and syllabus should be given as a process of strengthening, support and fortification.

Children already spend 6 to 9 hours in schools. Based on this along with level of the child time required for the homework needs to be decided. Remember students are dealing with many subjects. Homework is given in every subject. Per day subjects need to be decided for different levels which would be decided by coordinators of the school in coordination with concerned person meant for the job, the vice principal or the Principal as the case may be. Ideal step could be a weekly time table made to include all subjects, with at least two subjects per day. Time should be decided keeping in mind the levels of children. Less time for lower levels and more time for higher levels could be decided upon. The range of time selected as model would be in the range of 10 minutes to 1.30 to 2.00 hours.

Home work should be based on 'I do, I learn' and not on rote learning. It should be done by children and not by parents or any elders. How is it possible that students only will do homework joyfully? There is only one key to it. And that is, it should be fun doing it through and through. If it is FUN, the children get motivated and do it on their own, probably asking for some support wherever they get stuck. HOMEWORK should be such that it invariably contributes to the development of the child's personality in totality through languages, Mathematics, Sciences, Aesthetic, Ethical, creative etc.

Few points for consideration:

We need to keep our mind open to all possibilities. This will help us to be broadminded and inclusive. Any reasonable, rational and wise opinions should be taken in for consideration. Whatever we apply through our wisdom should be simple and practical for children to understand and apply. Homework should not be vast, crushing and devastating. Let us, as teachers, not be passionate and over excited in giving unreasonable homework. It should be evenhanded, fair and balanced. Ultimately homework should enhance Knowledge, Understanding and Application skills of children.

13.
TESTS & EXAMINATIONS

- **What are tests?**

- **What are examinations?**

- **Why are tests conducted?**

- **Why are examinations conducted?**

- **How are the tests conducted?**

- **How are the examinations conducted?**

The test is a tool to measure the knowledge level of our students and adjust the learning material accordingly with the purpose of our students improve their learning. An exam or the examination is more formal and it helps guage whether a student has passed or failed a class or course. It is also the benchmark to decide whether he needs to start the course or class all over again.

Critics have denounced regular exams and classroom testing as encouraging 'teaching-to-the-test' that leads to shallow, rote learning. But there is mounting evidence that taking tests can in fact improve recall, and help students apply existing knowledge to new contexts and situations.

The main types of exams that you will have to complete are:
- Essay exams

- Multiple choice exams.

- Open-book and take-home exams.

- Problem or case-based exams.

- Oral exams.

What are tests?

Assessment is a process by which information is obtained relative to some known objective or goal. Assessment is a broad term that includes testing. A test is a special form of assessment. In other words, all tests are assessments, but not all assessments are tests. Therefore, a test is a small assessment.

Quizzes and exams, short type and long type tests that teachers routinely use to check on students' learning are the most common—and frequent—tests your child takes in school. In addition to classroom tests, your child may take one or more standardized achievement tests that schools are required to give each year.

What is assessed, is how much a child has absorbed and how long it will stay in his memory that needs to be tested. This encompasses all points including the child's power of retaining what he or she has learnt.

Why are they conducted?

- **We <u>test</u> at the end of a lesson or unit. We <u>assess</u> progress at the end of a school year through testing.**

- **Test to know student's understanding of the topic.**

- **Test to know how much he has absorbed**

- **Test to find mistakes and misunderstandings.**

- **Test to bring in corrections and clarifications.**

This essentially helps to diagnose areas of improvement.

Tests objective is to measure the student performance. In this way, the process of testing uncovers the quality of a student's academic achievement. There are a number of reasons as to why teachers administer tests for students.

There are a number of reasons standardized testing is good:

- Standardized testing can provide benchmarks for parents and teachers.

- Standardized tests can help identify problem areas in individual students, as well as schools and curriculums. It provides guidelines for curriculum.

- Test is to know how much the child has understood or absorbed. Small or slip tests or surprise tests are very important as the teacher assesses her teaching by knowing how they have responded in the tests so that she/he can take more appropriate steps to make children understand or comprehend the lesson or topic better.

- These tests help the teachers to know mistakes or misunderstanding of the students. This will help them to take required ways to rectify or correct their understanding of the lesson with clarifications.

In this way we can diagnose a child's areas of improvement and help them.

How are tests conducted?

Tests need to be conducted both **oral and written form**.

How to go about it depends on the teacher, subject and the needs of the children.

1. **Slip tests.**

2. **Surprise tests.**

3. **Class tests.**

4. **Monthly tests.**

5. **Unit tests.**

Tests are conducted either orally or in written form. Teacher decides how to go about it. The following common methods of tests can be looked into.

- Slip tests are short written tests which give an idea of children's performance of their understanding the lesson.

- Class tests are that which a teacher tests children after completion of a lesson essentially to test their understanding to identify their areas of improvement and work towards their rectifications.

- Monthly tests cover the syllabus that is covered in a month for every subject. The child is in a position to face monthly test after all small tests. Learning the lesson after all corrections there is a boost in the performance of the child.

- Unit tests are in a way bi-monthly, as the syllabus completed comparatively is limited and needs proper preparation for better performance and perfect assessment of each child.

Tests – Format of Questions

1. **Portion for the test should be small.**

2. **Questions should be relevant to the topic.**

3. **Do not ask beyond the topic.**

4. **Questions are to be objective or pertaining to short answers.**

5. **Keep the time in mind while forming questions.**

6. **Let the questions be simple with appropriate terms like describe, explain, elaborate evaluate, analyze, assess, interpret etc.**

7. **Let the child get used to these terms relating to the subject.**

Format of Questions in the Question papers are extremely important as certain points need to be kept in mind. As the test is for just the lesson or lessons completed, the portion for the test should be small. Questions should be relevant to the topic and should not be beyond the topic taught. Questions should be either objective or should pertain to short answers. It is essential to keep the time factor in mind. Time allotted for the test should be appropriate to the answers expected. The words used in the questions should be appropriate, suitable, fitting or apt like explain, describe, elaborate or narrate etc.

What are Examinations?

- **In summary, we measure performance, we assess learning, and we evaluate results in terms of some set of criteria.**

- **<u>Assessment</u> refers to the collection of data.**

- **<u>Evaluation</u> refers to the comparison of data to a standard.**

- **We evaluate through assessment and examinations.**

- **<u>Examinations</u> are final.**

Every teaching institution has to have a system which measures the knowledge of the learner. A method or a technique to measure the learning of a child is the examination. In a way, we measure performance, we assess learning. But we evaluate results in terms of some set of criteria. There is a difference between an assessment and evaluation in terms of knowledge and learning. Assessment refers to the collection of data of a child's learning, where as evaluation refers to the comparison of data to a standard. Complete evaluation comprises of evaluation through assessment and examinations. Total appraisals through examinations are final. This simply means a child is assessed throughout the year along with final examination.

Why are they conducted?

A test or examination is an <u>assessment</u> intended to measure a test-taker's <u>knowledge</u>, <u>skill</u>, <u>aptitude</u>, <u>physical fitness</u>, or classification in

many other topics.

Objective of a test or examination is intended to measure a child's knowledge, skill, aptitude, physical fitness or classification of many other topics. Basically the purpose is an assessment to see if he/she is suitable to go ahead with further knowledge.

Many students are studying because of exams. ... Actually it promotes competition among students. It helps in developing one's personality and confidence. And exams have the major role in providing necessary qualities in life such as hard work, patience, creativeness and leadership.

Educators Accountability is ultimately considered as essential to the educational system. The objectivity of the standardized tests leads to the next reason they are important. Because of their objectivity and ability to measure student learning, standardized tests are useful tools for holding teachers, schools, and districts accountable for success or failure. Exams help us learn and digest information more easily. Because students are under pressure to get good grades, they strive to do their best. Without exams, students would be able to put off their revision and find it hard to keep up in class.

How are examinations conducted?

1. **Quarterly.**

2. **Half Yearly.**

3. **Yearly.**

4. **Semester wise.**

When we eat, we eat piece by piece or little by little in the form of morsels. We cannot eat all at one go. In the same way learning also happens in small steps. Level is based on age and teaching and learning takes place every day in small forms. In the same way, what is learnt is tested in steps as mind handles knowledge in a very organised manner and the very first thing is that it enters and gets absorbed in the mind slowly and steadily. Therefore we have examinations conducted in a timely ordered manner. They are usually conducted quarterly, half yearly, yearly and also semester wise.

Examinations – Format of Question papers

1. **Should cater to all levels of students.**

2. **40% of questions should cater to lower level children.**

3. **30% of questions should cater to medium level children.**

4. **30% of questions to higher level of children.**

It is very important to give great care to the format of question papers and have some criteria for writing one. Firstly, irrespective of levels of children attempting the exam, the question paper should cater to all levels. General guidance is that 40% of questions should cater to children who are below average. 30% of the question paper should cater to children of average level. 30% of questions should be for the above average level of students. Thus, even the below average too is in a position to get a passing percentage. Above average children any way can be expected to score higher percentages.

Importance of tests :

- **Tests are a medium to find how much a child has understood.**

- **Helps objective corrections and reinforcement.**

- **Test are timed so to assess a child in small timely manner**

- **To make a child understand thoroughly.**

- **Similar to feeding knowledge and information in morsels.**

Tests basically are a technique to improve children's learning. This is a medium to find how much a child has learnt. What are his shortcomings and how to make a child to go through corrections and reinforce the knowledge or leanings. Tests are small methods to assess the child in a small way. It helps making the child understand thoroughly due to repeated learning. Tests are tools to feed knowledge and information in the form of tiny morsels as mind cannot absorb all at one go.

Importance of Examinations:

- **Examinations are FINAL.**

- **No chance of corrections and reinforcement.**

- **It is the essence of assessment of performance throughout the year.**

- **It is the main part of a child's yearly evaluation.**

- **It decides major part of a child's performance.**

Examinations are always final. There is no chance of corrections or reinforcements. Exam is the ultimate essence of learning throughout the year. It the main part of a child's yearly evaluation which is inclusive of continuous assessment of his/her learning and how much the child is able to perform. Examination decides major part of child's performance. Grades do matter – although they are not a reflection of ability. In a system of entrenched social inequality, exam results are not an accurate reflection of ability, diligence or anything else they're assumed to measure. They do, however, matter.

Examinations - has it killed the education system?

In India especially, there are many exams annually. Student barely has any time for extracurricular activities. Most of the exams structure and design are not sufficient to evaluate the real capabilities of the student.

My take on this is yes and no.

Yes, examinations are a head ache for children as they over burdened and stressed.

No, because today not only schools and educationists but also parents also have become aware of this stress and burden and are looking out for solutions to reduce stress and learn in a very liberated environment and stress free atmosphere

A TEACHER'S ROLE

- **A teacher needs to be sensitive to a child's performance at every level.**

- **He or she needs to take a child by the hand and lead.**

- **Needs to help and facilitate through every test so that the child is prepared for examination.**

- **Teacher needs to work with the child like a friend.**

Let's examine, how a child needs to be treated by the teacher in today's educational environment. Examination blues are very common. No child enjoys examinations. In this context, a teacher's role becomes very crucial. He/She needs to be very sensitive to a child's performance at every level. Handholding of a child to lead him/her comfortably without stress and with confidence is the demand of the day. This is something to be absorbed at every step by the child and not at one go. Every test provides a step in releasing stress and increasing confidence gradually. After going through a number of tests, the child is prepared for the final examination. Therefore, a series of tests lead to an examination where the child is comfortable in facing a given exam. A good and a friendly teacher is not a demanding and commanding person. A teacher always needs to be a friend, guide and philosopher to his students. This helps in smooth communication between them to solve and find solution to any of the problems that children face and this becomes a firm step in building confidence in them to face the world at large with a strong and positive personality.

EXAMINATION BLUES

To understand examination blues, we need to understand the purpose of exams. The purpose of exams is not to create a kind of fear psychosis among those who write exams but to make them understand the need to know how much of the knowledge has been absorbed, understood and has increased the ability of the person in its application. This fear psychosis is caused in students as everything in today's purpose of exams is misunderstood in obtaining the marks. This understanding is lacking in majority of today's parents also. The victim is obviously the child or any student for that matter. Why do they occur? A simple answer is insufficient and inappropriate study. Perhaps those who study and are blessed with unbounded memory are those who are capable of hitting the lottery of marks with distinction. Sadly our system of examinations tests only the memory in its abundance. But God's plan is different. He has made each one of us unique and not everyone can win the lottery. It is as simple as that. The pressure of the vast syllabus, the high expectations of the parents and the schools to push the child to the edge and the uncertainty of meeting those expectations are some of the causes of this fear. The question is, the importance of marks or the understanding and the application of the knowledge. In many cases, marks cannot guarantee the student's capability. And yet, they are the indicators.

How can this be balanced? When it comes to the experiences, they are the cause of nervousness, sweating, rapid heartbeat, confusion and in the process memory loss, unorganised presentation etc. In extreme cases it can also lead to suicidal tendency. But nature has given us the power of overcoming these and coming out victorious in the majority of cases. We as students go through these experiences and the best part is each one of us is sailing in the same boat. That is the heartening part of it.

'I am not the only one in this journey.' This feeling brings warmth, confidence, hard work and the right kind of attitude towards preparation for the exam. Coming to the problem of tackling the fear, the role played by the parents, school, the state and last but not least the role of the teacher is very important. They can provide a kind of support to student's study and hard work like pillars of strength and confidence. Having a friendly attitude by parents and teachers is essential to have a smooth communication with the children. Having a balanced approach when it comes to health, studies, and games, entertainment with focused attention towards studies stressing the importance of intense and passionate hard work will certainly take children in the right direction. Each factor responsible should take the responsibility of taking care of the concerned child and automatically, the impact will be created. What it means is the role played by the state and its agencies at the high school, professional courses level in making policies that are relevant, practical and helpful to the students. In this process, apoliticization of the concerned agencies is essential and cannot be ruled out. Children are at school most of their student life. Keeping this in mind, it is necessary that the school should take care of the students in their educational areas which includes physical, emotional, social, moral, spiritual, aesthetic and ethical developments. The next element that constitutes this, is the role of the parents. They are like the foundation for a monument. If it is strong, then the chances of making an error in bringing up their child is minimal. Lastly, a teacher's support to the students who appear for examinations works like a miracle in reducing these examination blues. A student must have a genuine and burning desire to do well in the examinations. A positive attitude will certainly help. The school can programme itself to increase the number of examinations and tests as well. Psychologically, the more you face a situation, the lesser the fear and higher confidence it instills. This does apply to examinations. The more one appears for examinations, the easier it becomes to take them easily and not buoyed on by fear. Any examination blues can be converted to pleasant greens bringing in the cooler attitude towards examinations.

14.
EVALUATION IN SCHOOLS

<u>**Evaluation = Continuous Comprehensive Assessment**</u>

<u>**What is CCA?**</u>

A normal understanding is:

- **Performance in tests throughout the year.**
- **Performance in quarterly, half yearly, yearly or semester wise examinations.**
- **Performance in extracurricular activities.**
- **As reflected in report cards.**

The words in question tell us that any assessment or test evaluation that is continuous throughout the year. Understanding the concepts and the complete knowledge of any topic. In short, it is a broader assessment of a student. This unquestionably includes quarterly, half yearly, yearly or semester examinations. Yearly evaluation includes continuous performance throughout the year. Apart from this, it also includes added performances in extracurricular activities. A comprehensive assessment is reflected in report cards.

<u>**Equally important are:**</u>

- **Psychological Assessments,**

- **IQ Testing,**
- **Achievement Testing,**
- **Functional Assessments,**
- **Behavioural Assessments,**
- **Testing for Dyslexia**
- **Learning Disabilities.**

As the above points reflect, the right way of assessment includes all. On ground, it is hardly done so. Schools are not implementing all of these when it comes to reality. Rarely do one find genuine educationists using tests for IQ , Achievement, Behavioural assessments etc. Dyslexia and Learning disabilities are noticed at a very young level in the primary sections. These problems need to be addressed for rectification then and there. Schools should have these problems identified and corrections taken up earlier than later. Teachers with specific training should be employed to facilitate such children, corrections done.

<u>**Talented and Gifted:**</u>

- **There should be an innovative and unique approach to education.**
- **Providing superb opportunities for young people to explore diverse subjects in a challenging, creative environment.**
- **The structured everyday school environments can be very difficult for a gifted child.**
- **There are very few programs and private schools for children that are for talented and gifted child.**
- **There are even fewer programs for gifted children who are present with learning disabled.**
- **Young children who are gifted often are misdiagnosed as they can become bored very easily.**

- **Getting out of their seat and being fidgety is taken as a drawback in learning.**

LEARNING DISABILITIES:

Learning disabilities are disorders that affect the ability :

- **to understand**

- **use spoken or written language,**

- **do mathematical calculations,**

- **coordinate movements,**

- **or direct attention.**

Although learning disabilities occur in very young children, the disorders are usually not recognized until the child reaches school age.

DYSLEXIA:

"Dyslexia is a learning disorder that involves difficulty in reading due to problems identifying speech sounds and learning how they relate to letters and words (decoding). Also called reading disability, dyslexia affects areas of the brain that process language."

WHAT IS IT?

It deals with Behaviour, Health, Development and Personality

WHY DOES IT OCCUR?

Disorderly development of mental abilities of the child.

HOW DOES IT EXPRESS ITSELF?

Writing and Motor Skills:

- Trouble with writing or copying; pencil grip is unusual; handwriting varies or is illegible.

- Clumsy, uncoordinated, poor at ball or team sports; difficulties with fine and/or gross motor skills and tasks; prone to motion-sickness.

- Can be ambidextrous, and often confuses left/right, over/under.

Math and Time Management:

- Has difficulty telling time, managing time, learning sequenced information or tasks, or being on time.

- Computing math shows dependence on finger counting and other tricks; knows answers, but can't do it on paper.

- Can count, but has difficulty counting objects and dealing with money.

- Can do arithmetic, but fails word problems; cannot grasp algebra or higher math.

Memory and Cognition:

- Excellent long-term memory for experiences, locations, and faces.

- Poor memory for sequences, facts and information that has not been experienced.

- Thinks primarily with images and feeling, not sounds or words (little internal dialogue).

Conclusion:

Evaluation of a child to be wholesome throughout the year.

- It should cover all areas of academics which means curriculum of all subjects at different levels.

- It should be physical, emotional, social, intellectual, spiritual, aesthetic and ethical.

- A special touch should be given to children with learning disabilities.

145

SECTION – V
Constructive Deviation

15.
CONSTRUCTIVE DEVIATION

WHAT IS CONSTRUCTIVE DEVIATION? : --

Definition: As the phrase denotes, the mainstream of activity is deviated positively for a different kind of engagement where a child is happily prepared for the change.

Any person who is continuously involved in any activity needs a break or change of activity to be fresh when he is back to the same activity.

WHY SHOULD WE FOLLOW THIS?

- **For breaking monotony.**
- **To bring in freshness.**
- **Creating more interest.**
- **Involving into the mainstream learning freshly.**
- **By deviating the child's attention satisfaction is created.**
- **With happiness as base, a child's learning capacity increases.**
- **Understanding, absorbing better and better retention in memory without much effort.**

HOW SHOULD THIS BE CONDUCTED?

- **Games and Sports**

- **Music and Drama**

- **Computer based learning**

- **Learning in the natural environment (may be class under a tree)**

- **Nature walk**

- **Playing in the sand for small children**

- **Painting**

- **Craft work   etc.**

As mentioned above, these activities can be incorporated with proper syllabus in their lesson planning.

For example: stressing on the importance classical music, refining them in the games of interest, drama and plays and preparing them for the contests and competitions where they excel. Children can be involved in physical activities which will make them healthier. A healthy body is a healthy mind. Learning in natural environment probably involves nature walks, picnics etc.

- Role plays, storytelling and even singing can be a part of such deviations. Children with interest in particular areas can be encouraged to make a career out of it.

- Narrations of sceneries, incidences, experiences can be a matter of attraction for children to be in classes. In fact, they wait for classes in which teacher takes personal interest in conducting such classes which ultimately make children attend and be serious about their lessons too.

Today's problem is that children have no interaction with the five elements of life. Nature : Earth, Water, Fire, Air and Space. Students have have minimum interaction with nature. Most of the population are moving towards urban areas, where only concrete is available instead of mud. Water and air is highly polluted, and temperatures everywhere are increasing, leaving the nature intolerable. Children spend most of their time inside their schools or in coaching classes and tuition centers. After spending time continuously in such air-conditioned places, the need certainly is for change in activity. Perhaps a play ground, yoga activity, practicing some art like singing and dancing is necessary that would freshen up the children mentally and physically. We as adults also need it to break the monotony of work.

How can we help the child?

Hobbies are considered as waste of time. But it is not so. Any constructive deviation works magically to make ourselves fresh and bright and helps us to work with freshness and breaks monotony. These hobbies could be drawing, painting, singing, playing indoor and outdoor games or any other hobby for that matter.

We need to inculcate these hobbies as per their tastes and interests. Hobbies become a part of our dynamic living, to the extent that these hobbies help in becoming their careers and many times turn out to be an occupying strategy to better their pastime or even a source of earning.

The best way to empower Gurus is just to read the below poem and follow simple means of becoming a teacher of essence. As a father Lincoln gives tips to his son's teacher how to handle a child. This is the real core of becoming a good teacher. Every teacher must read the poem and follow the simple suggestions to teach these attributes to every child.

Lincoln's Letter to his Son's Teacher

Abraham Lincoln was one of the most renowned American Presidents and his writings have been popular among history. Here is one of his writings, which is in fact a letter to his son's teacher. In this letter, he asks his son's teacher to teach some attributes to his son, and the letter became a memorable piece of historical literature. Every father desires his son's teacher to learn these qualities and every teacher must read them:

Lincoln's Letter to his Son's Teacher

He will have to learn, I know,

that all men are not just,

all men are not true.

But teach him also that

for every scoundrel there is a hero;

that for every selfish Politician,

there is a dedicated leader...

Teach him for every enemy there is a friend,

Steer him away from envy,

if you can,

teach him the secret of

quiet laughter.

Let him learn early that

the bullies are the easiest to lick…

Teach him, if you can,

the wonder of books…

But also give him quiet time

to ponder the eternal mystery of birds in the sky,

bees in the sun,

and the flowers on a green hillside.

In the school teach him

it is far honourable to fail

than to cheat…

Teach him to have faith

in his own ideas,

even if everyone tells him

they are wrong…

Teach him to be gentle

with gentle people,

and tough with the tough.

Try to give my son

the strength not to follow the crowd

when everyone is getting on the band wagon…

Teach him to listen to all men…

but teach him also to filter

all he hears on a screen of truth,

and take only the good

that comes through.

Teach him if you can,

how to laugh when he is sad…

Teach him there is no shame in tears,

Teach him to scoff at cynics

and to beware of too much sweetness…

Teach him to sell his brawn

and brain to the highest bidders

but never to put a price-tag

on his heart and soul.

Teach him to close his ears

to a howling mob

and to stand and fight

if he thinks he's right.

Treat him gently,

but do not cuddle him,

because only the test

of fire makes fine steel.

Let him have the courage

to be impatient…

let him have the patience to be brave.

Teach him always

to have sublime faith in himself,

because then he will have

sublime faith in mankind.

This is a big order,

but see what you can do…

He is such a fine little fellow,

my son!

Ref: Lincoln's Letter to his Son's Teacher

EPILOGUE:

<u>INTRICACIES OF EDUCATION</u>

What is today's education all about?

The answer to this needs a complete analytical approach, keeping in view, the changed requirements and expectations of a student in the society. In other words, the learning should match with the needs of society, which is moving at an unimaginable speed to catch up globally. A school, which does not fight through this, does not rightfully survive. To live through this expectation that total development of a child both vertically and laterally or academically and supportive activities is essential. Nevertheless, academic highhandedness has to be accepted.

The right kind of atmosphere, which ultimately creates an ambience for nurturing the child, has to be widespread involving the right kind of resource persons and resource centres in the institution. Appropriate academic exposure through full-fledged libraries and Internet resource would certainly work wonders.

The growth of a child, on all four levels -physical, social, intellectual, and emotional and spiritual- is happening during the school years. The role and responsibility of an educational institution is tremendous at this juncture. That is where the significance of a school is upheld in the society. This responsibility makes its presence felt at every level from pre-primary to +2 standards. Creation of an appropriate ambience is essential for a complete development of the personality of students.

Providing and keeping handy loads of info on the subject and the topic at all levels by their teachers goes a long way in making right approach to learning. Handouts and worksheets would work well on drilling and practicing variety of exercises. Any methods of making the lesson interesting would enhance the probability of attracting the focused attention of Waverly minds. These presentations may be either visual or auditory. Teacher's contribution in the facilitating process is the ultimate, which builds in the confidence of students. An essential factor or role of a teacher in building up a total personality of the student throughout the schooling years whether it is physical, intellectual, emotional or spiritual, is very influential. The teacher has to play a better role at every level, the more the sensitivity the better the role would be.

Value based learning in the school acts as a binding factor in the formation of a strong character. This is like a psychological cushion in facing the ups and downs of life. This is the undercurrent of life in reality, which protects a student and boosts as a life skill to handle the highs and lows and sail smoothly.

Coming to the most disputed factor that is corporal punishment, legally it could be questioned. It could be the most uncivilized way of treating a student in a school. It not only hinders smooth learning process but also could act like something, which would encourage acquiring and cultivating a negative trend in the character as a result of hurt ego. The best way to counter such a situation is through love and counselling with firmness and to keep away from physical handling.

A child's thinking process should be encouraged to develop at the primary level. 25% of learning could be through self-thinking and expression and 75% could be through drills, worksheets and exercises. At the junior level it could be 50-50 and at the senior level one could balance it to 75-25%. Under no circumstance memory part of development should be ignored, as it is an essential part of our mind.

A serious thought to the above points and a right implementation on the part of the school managements would be very beneficial in the long run in providing the best of the student community to the society at large.